.

Richard Strauss's

Salome

OPERA CLASSICS LIBRARY™ SERIES

Edited by Burton D. Fisher
Principal lecturer, *Opera Journeys Lecture Series*

Opera Journeys™ Publishing   /   Miami, Florida

Opera Journeys™ Mini Guide Series
Opera Classics Library™ Series
Opera Journeys™ Libretto Series
A History of Opera: Milestones and Metamorphoses
Opera Classics Library Puccini Companion: the Glorious Dozen

<u>*OVER 60 TITLES AVAILABLE:*</u>

•L'Africaine •Abduction from the Seraglio •Aida • Andrea Chénier
•The Barber of Seville •La Bohème •Boris Godunov • Carmen
•Cavalleria Rusticana • Così fan tutte •Der Freischütz •Der Rosenkavalier
•Die Fledermaus •Don Carlo •Don Giovanni •Don Pasquale •The Elixir of Love
•Elektra •Eugene Onegin •Exploring Wagner's Ring •Falstaff
•La Fanciulla del West •Faust •La Fille du Régiment •Fidelio
•The Flying Dutchman •Gianni Schicchi • Hansel and Gretel
•L'Italiana in Algeri •Julius Caesar •Lohengrin
•Lucia di Lammermoor •Macbeth • Madama Butterfly •The Magic Flute
•Manon •Manon Lescaut •The Marriage of Figaro •A Masked Ball
•The Mikado •Norma •Otello •I Pagliacci •Pelléas et Mélisande
•Porgy and Bess •The Rhinegold •Rigoletto •The Ring of the Nibelung
•La Rondine •Salome •Samson and Delilah •Siegfried •La Sonnambula
•Suor Angelica •Il Tabarro •The Tales of Hoffmann •Tannhäuser •Tosca
•La Traviata •Tristan and Isolde •Il Trittico •Il Trovatore •Turandot
•Twilight of the Gods •The Valkyrie •Werther •Wozzeck

WEB SITE: www.operajourneys.com   E MAIL: operaj@bellsouth.net

Contents

a *prelude........*

to OPERA CLASSICS LIBRARY's

Salome

Richard Strauss's *Salome* is a masterpiece of the lyric theater, a work of exceptional orchestral power and brilliance, that is integrated with audacious harmonic adventurism; and in 1905, its premiere year, its daring musical eroticism was considered obscene.

OPERA CLASSICS LIBRARY explores Strauss's masterful one-act opera. There is a *Commentary and Analysis* that provides insightful drama and character analysis, together with the *Principal Characters, Brief Synopsis,* and *Story Narrative with Music Highlight Examples.*

The *Libretto* for *Salome* has been newly translated by the Opera Journeys staff with specific emphasis on retaining a literal translation, but also with the objective to provide a faithful translation in modern and contemporary English; in this way, the substance of the opera becomes more intelligible. To enhance educational and study objectives, the *Libretto* contains musical highlight examples interspersed within the drama's exposition. In addition, the text includes a selected *Discography, Videography,* and a *Dictionary of Opera and Musical Terms.*

The opera art form is the sum of many artistic expressions: theatrical drama, music, scenery, poetry, dance, acting and gesture. In opera, it is the composer who is the dramatist, using the emotive power of music to express intense, human conflicts. Words evoke thought, but music provokes feelings; opera's sublime fusion of words, music, and all the theatrical arts provides powerful theater, an impact on one's sensibilities that can reach into the very depths of the human soul.

Strauss's *Salome* is certainly a magnificent operatic invention, a towering tribute to the art form as well as to its ingenious composer.

Burton D. Fisher
Editor
OPERA CLASSICS LIBRARY

Salome

Opera in German in one act

Music
by
Richard Strauss

Libretto based on Hedwig Lachmann's abridged German translation of Oscar Wilde's play, *Salome*

**Premiere: Königliches Opernhaus
Dresden, 1905**

Principal Characters in Salome

Herod Antipas, Tetrarch of Judaea	Tenor
Herodias, Herod's wife	Mezzo-soprano
Salome, daughter of Herodias	Soprano
Jokanaan, the Prophet (John the Baptist)	Baritone
Narraboth, a young Syrian Captain of the Royal Guard	Tenor
A Page of Herodias	Contralto
Five Jews	four tenors, one bass
Two Nazarenes	Tenor, Bass
Two Soldiers	Basses
A Cappadocian	Tenor
Herod's Page	Tenor (or Soprano)

TIME: Beginning of the 1st century, during the lifetime of Christ

PLACE: Herod's palace in ancient Palestine

Brief Story Synopsis

Herod Antipas, Tetrarch, or Governor of Judaea, is celebrating his birthday at a banquet at his palace. From a terrace outside, Narraboth, the Captain of the Guard, observes Salome, Herod's beautiful stepdaughter, who is inside the hall: he expresses his uncontrollable yearning and passion for her. Irritated by Herod and the guests, Salome leaves the banquet and appears on the terrace. She hears the voice of Jokanaan, the Hebrew Prophet (John the Baptist), announcing the Messianic Deliverance; the Prophet has been imprisoned in a cistern because Herod fears he will propagate unrest.

Salome becomes fascinated by the Prophet's voice and requests that she see him, but the Soldiers advise her that Herod's orders forbid it. Salome becomes obsessed. She succeeds in getting her wish fulfilled by promising favors to the lovesick Narraboth. Jokanaan emerges from the cistern: he denounces not only Herod, but also Herodias, Salome's mother, for the sin of marrying her dead husband's brother.

Salome becomes infatuated with the Prophet and pleads for a kiss: he contemptuously refuses her, cursing her when he learns that she is the daughter of the iniquitous Herodias. Narraboth, finding their interchange unbearable, kills himself.

Herod and Herodias quarrel: she is jealous of Herod's lust for her daughter Salome, and demands that Jokanaan be killed because he insulted her. Herod is in awe of the Prophet and fears a religious uprising if he harms him.

Herod, lusting for Salome, offers her any wish if she dances for him. Salome agrees to dance, afterwards demanding that Herod fulfill his promise by giving her the head of Jokanaan as her reward.

The executioner delivers the decapitated head of the Prophet to Salome, who erupts into ecstatic rapture and uncontrollable passion as she kisses it. The shocked and disgusted Herod orders his guards to crush Salome to death.

Story Narrative and Music Highlight Examples

There is no overture to *Salome*. The curtain rises immediately to a three-bar theme associated with Salome.

Salome motive:

It is night, and the moon shines very brightly on a broad terrace of Herod's palace. Inside, a banquet celebrates Herod's birthday, the Tetrarch entertaining Roman envoys with whom he is anxious to ingratiate himself, Egyptian ambassadors, and Jewish zealots, who from time-to-time quarrel violently about biblical doctrine.

Narraboth, a young Syrian recently appointed by Herod as captain of the guard, stands on the terrace and stares fixedly into the banquet hall. He expresses his infatuation, yearning, and love for Princess Salome: "Wie schön ist die Prinzessin Salome heute Abend!" ("How beautiful Princess Salome is tonight!")

Narraboth's infatuation with Salome:

The Page senses foreboding and premonitions of danger when he notices the moon turning dark and shadowy: "See how strange the moon looks! She looks like a woman rising from a tomb."

The Page tries in vain to distract Narraboth's attention from Princess Salome: "You're always looking at her. You look at her too much. It's dangerous to look at people in such a way. Something terrible will happen."

But Narraboth is intransigent, infatuated and lovesick: he praises Salome's beauty, but is perturbed that she seems so pale in the bright moonlight.

Two Soldiers guard the cistern where Jokanaan is imprisoned. Herod fears that the Prophet's religious fervor will foment unrest, and he has forbidden anyone to see him.

An uproar is heard from the banquet hall. The rival Jewish sects are arguing, their disagreements erupting into temper tantrums: the Pharisees staunchly claim that angels exist; and the Sadducees declare that angels are nonexistent. The Soldiers on the terrace comment about their arguments with cynical detachment: "The Jews. They never change; they're always arguing about their religion."

Narraboth, oblivious to the tumult inside, remains infatuated with Salome and continues to praise her beauty: he rhapsodizes again that he has never seen her look so pale, and that her face is like the shadow of a rose reflected in a silver mirror.

"Wie schön ist die Prinzessin Salome heute Abend!"

NARRABOTH

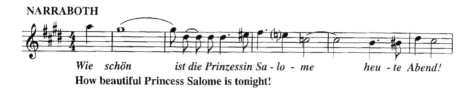

Wie schön   ist die Prinzessin Sa - lo - me   heu - te Abend!
How beautiful Princess Salome is tonight!

Again, the apprehensive Page expresses his anxiety, warning Narraboth to restrain his fatal infatuation with Salome: that it is hazardous for him to continue staring lustfully at the Princess. The Soldiers, observing the banquet inside, comment that Herod appears gloomy, his eyes fixed on someone, but they cannot see whom: it is Salome.

Jokanaan's voice is heard from the depths of the cistern, solemnly and majestically declaring his impassioned prophecy of the Messianic Deliverance: "Nach mir wird Einer kommen, der ist stärker aks ich." ("After me shall come another who is stronger than I. I am not worth to undo the laces of His shoes. When He comes, all the desolate places shall rejoice. When He comes, the eyes of the blind shall see the day. When He comes, the ears of the deaf shall be opened."

One of the Soldiers, weary of the Prophet's fanatic wailing, suggests that they silence him forcibly. But another Soldier speaks tenderly about the holy man, commenting that he is a gentle being who thanks him each day after he brings him his food. Then he responds to the inquiries of a Cappadocian, explaining that the Prophet comes from the desert where crowds of people flocked to him. He was clothed in camel's hair, fed on locusts, and preached to his young disciples: fearing unrest, the Tetrarch imprisoned him in the cistern, isolated so that no one may see him.

Narraboth, whose eyes have remained fixed on the banquet hall, erupts into excitement when he notices Salome rising from her seat and exiting the hall: he comments that she appears agitated, like a straying dove. The Page again implores Narraboth not to look at her.

Salome appears on the terrace in a state of excitement and agitation.

Salome emerges from the banquet:

Salome is distraught and angry, bewildered by her stepfather, Herod, because he stares at her with such lust in his eyes: "with his mole's eyes under his shaking eyelids." The banquet became unbearable for Salome: she became irritated by the uncouth and barbaric Romans, the foolish squabbling among the Jews, and the crafty quietness of the Egyptians.

Having escaped from the banquet, Salome welcomes the fresh air outside, and delights in the brightness of the moon: "She is like a silver flower, cold and chaste. Yes, there is a youthful beauty about the moon, a virgin's beauty."

Narraboth's infatuation with Salome remains undaunted. The Page expresses his apprehension: "Something terrible will happen. Why do you look at her like that?"

For the first time, Salome hears the Prophet's voice resounding from the cistern: "Behold, the Lord has come: the Son of Man has come."

Jokanaan's theme:

Solemnly

Salome questions the Soldiers about the voice she hears. A Soldier tells her that it is the Prophet, and Salome immediately deduces that it is "he of whom the Tetrarch is so frightened." And, she realizes that he is the holy man who has condemned her mother as a depraved and incestuous adulteress.

Salome's curiosity about the Prophet becomes aroused: Narraboth pleads with her to return to the banquet, but she is heedless to his pleas and disregards him.

A slave announces that Herod has commanded Salome to return to the banquet. Salome brushes him aside and bluntly refuses, immediately directing her attention to the Prophet. She asks the Soldier: "Is this Prophet an old man?", and he replies that he is quite young.

Once more, the Prophet's solemn voice is heard from the cistern: "Do not rejoice, land of Palestine, just because the rod that beat him is broken. For a basilisk shall come from the seed of the serpent; its offspring shall devour the birds."

The strangeness of the Prophet's voice and the enigma of his message inflame Salome with curiosity. Salome announces that she wants to speak with the Prophet. The second Soldier, agitated and apprehensive, tells her that the Tetrarch has commanded that no one, not even the High Priest, may see the Prophet. But Salome does not fear Herod, and her relentless obsession intensifies. She commands the Soldier: "I want to speak to him. Have this Prophet brought out!"

Both Soldiers try to reason with Salome, fearful of disobeying Herod's orders that no one be allowed to speak to the Prophet. Salome approaches the cistern, peers down into its recesses, and becomes horrified: "How dark it is down there! It must be terrible to live in such a black pit. It's just like a tomb!" Salome becomes insistent. She turns to the Soldiers, her anger intensifying, and again commands them to bring the Prophet to her so that she may look at him. The Soldiers, shuddering in fear, again refuse.

Salome, overcome with desire, is dismayed that her will is being frustrated. With devious artfulness, she exploits Narraboth's weakness and hopeless devotion to her and proceeds to weave her spell on him: she wields her erotic power, cajoles him, and promises him that if he lets her see the Prophet, when she passes him tomorrow at the city gates she will throw him a flower, glance at him through her veil, and smile upon him.

Narraboth finds himself in conflict: his emotions are overpowering his reason. At first he protests to Salome, invoking the Tetrarch's orders that no one raise the cover of the cistern; it is forbidden to see the Prophet, and he dare not disobey. But Narraboth's resolution falters, and he surrenders to his lust for Salome. Finally, unable to conquer his emotions, he issues the order: "Let the Prophet out. Princess Salome wishes to see him."

As the face of the moon suddenly becomes obscured, Jokanaan emerges from the cistern: all remain immobilized and in tense expectancy, the music exploding with a collision of themes representing Jokanaan's piety and Salome's passion.

Jokanaan emerges from the cistern:

Jokanaan ferociously launches a tirade against the evil acts of Herod: his lust, iniquities, sins, depravity, and incest; "Wo ist er, dessen Sündenbecher jetzt voll ist?" ("Where is he whose cup of sin overflows? Where is he, who, wearing a silver robe, will one day die before all people?") He commands everyone to heed the call of the Messianic Deliverance, seek salvation, and redeem themselves through repentance.

Salome and Jokanaan confront each other for the first time, a collision of the sacred with the profane. She is breathless at the first sight of the Prophet, repelled yet overcome with fascination, desire, and lust. She immediately surrenders to an incomprehensible fatal attraction for the Prophet, a combination of physical longing and compulsive desire.

Salome's desire and lust:

Jokanaan denounces Herodias, Salome's mother: "Wo ist sie die sich hingab der Lust ihrer Augen" ("Where is she, who surrendered to the lust in her eyes.") The Prophet continues: "Where is she who gave herself to the leaders of Assyria? Where is she who gave herself to the young men of Egypt, with their fine linens and precious jewels, their golden shields and bodies like giants?" The Prophet urges Herodias to "rise from her bed of incest, the bed of her abominations, so that she may hear the words of the One who prepares the way of the Lord, and that she may repent for her sins."

Although the Prophet has been condemning her mother, Salome erupts into childish excitement, intoxicated by unconscious desires and a pathologic sensuality. Ironically, she recoils from the Prophet: "He is terrifying. He is really terrifying."

Salome's infatuation:

The despairing Narraboth urges Salome to leave the terrace, but she heeds him not, captivated by the Prophet, and desiring that he speak again.

Salome studies the body of the Prophet, discovering that he is neither young nor fervent, but a gaunt and dreadful man. Nevertheless, she has become subconsciously captivated by him: "He's like an ivory statue. I'm sure he's as chaste as the moon. His flesh must be as cool as ivory. I must look closer at him!"

Jokanaan fixes his attention on Salome and inquires: "Wer ist dies Weib, das mich ansieht?" ("Who is this woman looking at me?") The Prophet forbids her to look at him. Then Salome proudly identifies herself: "I am Salome, the daughter of Herodias, the Princess of Judaea." Jokanaan realizes that he is in the presence of evil and promptly condemns the daughter of the dissolute Herodias: "Your mother has filled the earth with the wine of her iniquities, and God has heard the cry of her sins."

Salome remains calm, oblivious to the Prophet's denunciation of her mother; the Prophet's words merely inspire the unconscious perversity in Salome's mind. She replies casually and childishly to the Prophet: "Speak again, Jokanaan, your voice is like music to my ears." Salome has become completely obsessed by the Prophet's tirades and asks him what she must do?

Jokanaan denounces Salome as the "daughter of Sodom," commanding her away from him, and urging her to seek salvation: she must cover her face with a veil, scatter ashes on her head, and "go into the wilderness and seek the Son of Man." Salome inquires: "Who is He, the Son of Man? Is He as beautiful as you, Jokanaan?" Salome's erotic determination inflames the Prophet: he tells her that doom awaits Herod and Herodias; he can hear the "beating of the wings of the angel of death in the palace."

Narraboth again pleads with Salome to return to the banquet, but she is undeterred and ignores him: her monomania explodes as she confesses her lust and love for the Prophet: "Jokanaan! I am in love with your body." The more violent Jokanaan's denunciations, the more infatuated and fascinated Salome becomes, her unconscious cravings, compulsions, and amorous obsessions for him exploding into ecstatic rapture.

Salome is now completely dominated by her perverse passion for the Prophet: she praises Jokanaan by conjuring up sensual images of his body: "Your body is as white as the lilies of a field that have not been mowed. Your body is as white as the snows on the mountains of Judaea. The roses in the gardens of the Queen of Arabia are not as white as your body, nor the roses in the garden of Arabia's Queen, when the leaves fall at dawn, nor the moon when she lies on the sea. There is nothing in this world as white as your body."

Salome's obsession for Jokanaan reaches an impassioned climax: "Let me touch your body."

Jokanaan rejects Salome. He further condemns her, exhorting the "daughter of Babylon" that "evil came into the world by woman." The Prophet is appalled and refuses to hear her voice: "I listen only to the voice of the Lord God."

The Prophet's rejection of Salome further inflames her relentless desire for him, but now his denunciations incite her to revenge: in an instant, Salome's fascination with the Prophet turns to revulsion. Salome's will has been defeated and she condemns the prophet: "Your body is hideous. It is like the body of a leper. It is like a plastered wall where snakes have crawled, where scorpions have made their nest! It is like a whitened sepulcher full of loathsome things. It is horrible, your body is horrible."

But just as suddenly, Salome resumes her lust and yearning for the Prophet. She again expresses her compulsive desire for him, this time, evoking the beauty of his hair: "It is your hair that I love, Jokanaan. Your hair is like bunches of grapes, like bunches of black grapes that hang from the vine trees of Edom. Your hair is like the mighty cedars of Lebanon, which give shade to lions and robbers. The long black nights, when the moon hides her face, and the stars are afraid, are not as black as your hair. The silence of forests. Nothing in the world is as black as your hair. Let me touch your hair!"

Jokanaan thunders a new wave of revulsions and harsh rebuffs at Salome, bidding this daughter of Sodom to stand back, to leave him and not profane "the temple of the Lord." But his rejection merely provokes Salome to renew her frenzied attack on him: "Your hair is horrible! It is thick with dirt and dust. It is just like a crown of thorns on your head. It is like a knot of black serpents writhing around your neck. I do not like your hair."

Salome's irreversible and obsessive craving intensifies, expressed by her in frenzied imagery: "It is your mouth I desire, Jokanaan. Your mouth is like a band of scarlet on a tower of ivory. It is like a pomegranate cut with an ivory knife. The pomegranates that bloom in the garden of Tyre, redder than roses, are not so red. The red fanfares that herald the approach of Kings in wartime and place fear in the enemy, are not as red as your mouth. Your mouth is redder than the feet of those who tread the wine, stamping in the wine presses. It is redder than the feet of the doves that haunt the holy. Your mouth is like a branch of coral found in the twilight sea; it is like vermilion that Kings take from the mines of Moab. There is nothing in the world as red as your mouth."

Salome's infatuation and obsession with the Prophet reaches a climactic tempest of exploding passions as she expresses her yearning to kiss Jokanaan: "Let me kiss your mouth!" Jokanaan again vehemently rejects her: "Never, daughter of Babylon! Daughter of Sodom! Never!"

Over and over again, Salome repeats her monomania: "Ich will deinen Mund küssen, Jokanaan!" ("I will kiss your mouth, Jokanaan.")

" Ichwill deinen Mund küssen"

Salome, consumed by her desire for the Prophet, is blind and oblivious to what is happening around her. Narraboth, watching her in horror, tries repeatedly to deter her and compel her to reason, but she ignores him. The Captain, possessed and desperately in love with the unattainable Princess, can no longer endure listening to Salome's craving for the Prophet: in despair and jealousy, he stabs himself, his body falling between Salome and the Prophet.

Oblivious to Narraboth's suicide, the morbid passion of a depraved teenager collide with the pious exhortations of the Prophet. Jokanaan denounces Salome as an accursed daughter of adultery who must seek salvation and redemption by finding Him: "Go, seek Him! He is in a boat on the Sea of Galilee talking with His disciples. Kneel down on the shore of the sea, and call Him by name. When He comes to you, and He comes to all who call Him, bow down before Him, and ask for remission of your sins."

But Salome, sensually intoxicated and obsessed with lust for the Prophet, is oblivious to salvation. She is possessed by her idee fixe and continues her plea to Jokanaan, repeating it over and over again: "Let me kiss your mouth, Jokanaan!" And Jokanaan continues to reject her: "Sei verflucht, Tochter der blutschänderischen Mutter. Sei verflucht." ("You are accursed, daughter of an incestuous mother. You are accursed.")

As Jokanaan descends back into the cistern, the orchestra collides with Salome's theme of desire and Jokanaan's themes of the Messianic Deliverance, a musical tension between the sacred and the profane, and the spirit and the flesh. As Jokanaan disappears into the darkness, Salome stands before the cistern, frustrated, yearning, and longing.

Herod arrives, lustfully pursuing Salome: "Wo ist Salome? Wo ist die Prinzessin?" ("Where is Salome? Where is the Princess?") He is a neurasthenic beset by fears and insecurities, and now under the influence of too much wine. Herodias accompanies him, enraged with jealousy at her husband's overt lust for her daughter; she urges him to return to the banquet and to cease pursuing Salome with such obsessive lust.

Herod immediately becomes apprehensive and paranoid by omens, the dark night sky arousing a neurotic consciousness of something sinister: "The moon looks so strange tonight! Doesn't she have a strange look? She is like a mad woman, looking everywhere for lovers. She reels through the clouds like a drunken woman." Herodias replies to her besotted husband contemptuously: "No, the moon is like the moon, that's all. Let's go inside."

But Herod is dauntless in his pursuit of Salome. He orders torches and tables brought to the terrace: he will drink again to honor Caesar's ambassadors, but with Salome at his side. Herod stumbles after slipping on blood. He inquires about the blood, and then sees a corpse. A Soldier advises him that it is Narraboth, the captain of the guard. But Herod becomes confused because he gave no order for anyone to be killed. The Soldiers inform him that Narraboth committed suicide.

Narraboth's death causes Herod to suddenly becomes possessed by fear and overcome by foreboding: he feels cold and believes that a chill wind blows; and he imagines that there are sudden gusts, the beating of the huge wings of the angel of death. He concludes that Narraboth's death was Divine justice because the Captain, like Herod, looked lustfully at Salome. Nervous, apprehensive, and perturbed, Herod orders Narraboth's body removed from the terrace.

Herodias again pleads with Herod to return to the banquet, explaining that he seems ill. But Herod rejects his wife, his entire thoughts focused on Salome. He comments that he finds Salome pale, perhaps sick. He orders his wine cup replenished and tries to persuade Salome to share wine with him, longing to watch her "dip her little red lips into it."

"Salome, komm, trink Wein mit mir"

Molto animato
HEROD

Sa - lo - me, komm, trink Wein   mit mir,
Salome, come drink wine with me,

But Salome's inner thoughts are concerned with her unconscious passions for the Prophet. She coldly refuses him: "I am not thirsty, Tetrarch." Herod turns to Herodias, reproaching her for her daughter's refusal. But Herodias defends her daughter and again rebukes Herod for lustfully gazing at her daughter.

Herod attempts to lure Salome by offering to share fruit with her: "I love to see your little bite marks in a sweet fruit." Again, Salome refuses, telling him quietly, "I am not hungry, Tetrarch." And again, Herod blames Herodias for rearing Salome so poorly. But this time Herodias confronts Herod acrimoniously, reminding him that she and her daughter are descendants of a royal race; his father was a camel driver, and a thief and robber.

Herod renews his entreaties, this time offering to place Salome on her mother's throne beside him. Salome grimly replies, "I am not tired, Tetrarch."

From the depths of the cistern, Jokanaan's voice resounds again with his annunciation: "The time has come; the day of which I spoke is here." Herodias erupts in anger, ordering Herod to silence the fanatic man who continues to insult her. But Herod refuses, defending the man as a great Prophet; besides, he admonishes Herodias, "He has said nothing against you." Herodias accuses Herod of being afraid of the Prophet, but Herod defends himself as fearless of any man. If he is not afraid of the Prophet, Herodias suggests, "why don't you give him to the Jews, who have been screaming for him for months?" But Herod refuses, defending the Prophet: "He is a holy man. He is a man who has seen God."

The Jews erupt into furious arguments over religious dogma, the first Jew arguing that the Messiah is yet to come; he condemns Jokanaan as a false Prophet, not the incarnation of the Prophet Elijah who was the last prophet to see God. The second argues that perhaps Elijah never saw God but only His shadow. The third asserts that God shows Himself at all times and in everything: in what is good as well as evil. The fourth concludes that the others speak very dangerous dogma that emanates from Alexandria, from the Greeks and Gentiles. And the fifth admonishes that God operates in mysterious ways. The cacophony upsets Herodias, who pleads that Herod quiet the Jews.

Tempers and temperatures rise when Jokanaan's voice again announces the Messianic Deliverance: "So the day is come, the day of the Lord, and I can hear in the mountains the feet of Him, who will be the Savior of the world." Herod inquires the meaning of "Savior of the world," causing a Nazarene to announce that the Messiah has come, which is emphatically denied by the First Jew. The Nazarene defends his proclamation, describing how "He works miracles everywhere. He changed water into wine at a wedding in Galilee. He healed two lepers at Capernaeum. He also healed blind people. And he was seen on a mountain talking with angels!"

Herodias denounces the miracles as nonsense, but Herod turns to fear when the other Nazarene reveals that the Messiah raised the daughter of Jairus from the dead. Herod praises the miracles but expresses dread at the idea of the dead coming to life again: "I forbid him to do that. It would be dreadful if the dead came to life again!" Nevertheless, Herod is both inquisitive and doubtful, deciding that this Messiah of whom they speak must be found.

The commotion becomes dominated by the voice of Jokanaan —— heard from the cistern —— heaping fresh curses on Herodias, denouncing her, and predicting her imminent death: "The harlot, that daughter of Babylon, thus speaks the Lord, our God. A multitude will rise against her and take stones and stone to death. Their captains will pierce her with their sharp swords and crush her beneath their heavy shields. And thus I will wipe out all wickedness from the earth, and all women shall learn not to imitate her abominations."

Herodias, who was initially coldly aloof from the tumult, becomes infuriated by Jokanaan's abuse and loses her self control: she screams that the Prophet is outrageous, that Herod has allowed him to speak scandalously against her, and that Herod must silence him. Casually, Herod replies that the Prophet did not mention her by name.

Jokanaan continues, forecasting the horrible punishment of sinners: "On that day the sun shall turn black as sackcloth, and the moon shall become like blood, and the stars shall fall to the earth like ripe figs from the fig tree. On that day, the kings of the earth shall be afraid."

Herodias condemns the Prophet, and again urges Herod to silence him. But Herod is consumed with but one obsession and desire; he insists that Salome dance for him. And he is oblivious to Herodias, who states emphatically: "I will not have her dancing." To the delight of her mother, Salome refuses to dance.

While Salome broods over the cistern, Jokanaan's voice thunders again with his prediction of the Messianic Deliverance. Herod, desperate and impassioned, again begs Salome to dance for him, but this time he promises her anything she desires: "If you dance for me you may ask of me what ever you want. I'll give you what you ask for." Salome suddenly becomes aroused: "Will you really give me whatever I ask, Tetrarch?" Herodias commands her daughter not to dance, but Salome is heedless. Obsessed and determined, Herod makes a bold promise to Salome if she dances for him: "Everything, everything, that you ask for, even half my kingdom."

Salome makes Herod confirm his promise by an oath: by his life, crown and gods. Suddenly Herod becomes overwhelmed with portents and senses a chill wind and the beating of unseen wings: "Ah! It is as though there's a huge black bird: is it hovering over the terrace?" He shivers and erupts into a fever, and to cool himself, calls for water, snow to eat, and the loosening of his cloak. But he realizes that it his crown, decorated with festive garlands of roses, that is suffocating him; he removes it, recovers from his seizure, and immediately resumes his relentless request that Salome dance for him.

Herodias makes one last attempt to prevent Salome from dancing. She protests with fury and outrage, maddened and confounded by the voice of Jokanaan accusing Herod's court of gross immorality. In vain, she again demands that Herod accompany her inside. But Herod will remain because he has triumphed. Salome will dance for him: "Ich bin bereit, Tetrarch" ("I am ready, Tetrarch.")

The *Dance of the Seven Veils* represents Salome's exotic and sinuous evocations of her teenage erotic fantasies and desires that she will use to inflame the lascivious Herod.

At first, the music is a lulling and insinuating oriental theme.

Dance of the Seven Veils - First theme:

Then the mood changes to luxurious melodiousness.

Dance of the Seven Veils - Second theme:

At one point, Salome seems tired and faint from the wild rhythms of the dance, but she collects herself and resumes with renewed strength; as she dances, she pauses by the cistern like a visionary, her thoughts concentrating on Jokanaan. Then, the music of the dance erupts into a semi-barbaric wildness, Salome making convulsive gestures, and concluding by throwing herself at Herod's feet.

After Salome's dance, Herod is exhilarated and excited. He turns triumphantly to Herodias: "You see, your daughter has danced for me!" Herod quickly invites Salome to come near to him so that he can grant her the promised reward: "Tell me what you want? Speak!" Salome kneels before him humbly, but responds coldly: "I want someone to bring me on a silver platter.... the head of Jokanaan." ("Den Kopf des Jochanaan.") The revenge-lusting Herodias becomes delighted and commends her daughter's request: for Herodias, the prophet who condemned her will now be destroyed and she will avenge his condemnation of her.

But Herod is appalled, urging Salome to refute her mother, the woman who has always given her bad advice. Salome replies firmly, stating that she does not listen to her mother and has asked for the Prophet's head for her own pleasure. Herod tries to dissuade Salome, imploring her to choose something else. Herodias defends Salome and urges her to remain firm; death to the man who has scandalized her.

Herod pleads with Salome, expressing his horror at the idea of a decapitated head as her reward. He tries to reason with Salome, offering her fabulous jewels, or anything in his kingdom: the finest emerald in the world, his beautiful white peacocks. Herodias reminds him that he must abide by his oath; Herod immediately silences her.

Herod tries to reason with Salome, but she remains intransigent, adamant and steadfast, making her request with increasing fury: "Gib mir den Kopf des Jochanaan!" ("Give me the head of Jokanaan!") Herodias again praises her daughter's determination. Herod turns to Salome and again tries to reason with her, terrified because he believes that the Prophet is a holy man sent by God and he fears God's anger; if Herod has him killed something terrible would happen to him. But he fears even more the misfortune that will overcome him if he does not honor his oath.

Salome remains undaunted. Herod continues to try to dissuade her with more offers: pearls, topazes, opals, and other priceless treasures. He will give Salome all, even the cloak of the High Priest, but not the life of the Prophet. But Herod has become helpless, frustrated in his hopeless attempt to dissuade Salome from her desires. In despair, he accedes to Salome and issues the order: "Man soll ihr geben, was sie verlangt! Sie ist in Wahrheit ihrer Mutter Kind!" ("Let her be given what she wants! She is indeed her mother's child!")

While Herod remains spellbound and in shock, Herodias takes advantage of his collapse and removes the Ring of Death from his finger. She gives it to a soldier, who immediately gives it to Naaman, the executioner, who, upon receiving it, descends into the cistern. Herod notices that his Ring is gone, and inquires who has taken it. Herodias replies savagely that it is being used to satisfy her daughter's request: "My daughter has done well!" Herod remains dumbfounded, certain that misfortune will overcome them.

Salome leans over the cistern, listening intently in tense expectation to hear Jokanaan's cries and struggles; she is confounded that she does not hear screams or a struggle from a man about to be killed. She calls for the executioner to strike, but there is only a terrible silence. She hears what she believes is the executioner's sword falling and concludes that he is a coward, afraid to behead the Prophet. Salome turns hysterically to Herodias's Page and threatens him if he does not command the soldiers to descend into the cistern and bring her what she desires, what was promised to her by the Tetrarch, what is hers. The Page recoils in horror. Salome herself turns to the soldiers and orders them into the cistern, calling to Herod to command them to bring her the head of Jokanaan.

As Salome eagerly awaits her prize, amid almost unbearable orchestral tension, the executioner's huge black arm rises from the cistern bearing the head of Jokanaan on a silver shield. In her moment of triumph and ecstasy Salome seizes the head: Herod hides his face in his cloak; Herodias smiles as she delivers a platter for the head; the Nazarenes fall on their knees and begin to pray. Salome has avenged Jokanaan's humiliation and rejection of her: she is victorious and has overpowered the Prophet. Herod is repelled and fearful, but Herodias gloats in victory. Salome's passions intensify and explode, the fulfillment of her neurotic and erotic obsession for the Prophet."

Salome explodes in triumph as she addresses the Prophet's severed head: "Ah, You wouldn't let me kiss your mouth, Jokanaan! Well, I will kiss it now! I will sink my teeth into it, as one bites a ripe fruit. Yes. I will kiss your mouth, Jokanaan. I said I would, didn't I say it?"

Salome rhapsodizes to the Jokanaan's decapitated head: "But why don't you look at me, Jokanaan? Your eyes that were so terrible, so full of rage and scorn, are shut now. Why are they closed? Open your eyes! Lift up your eyelids Jokanaan. Why don't you look at me? Are you afraid of me, Jokanaan, that you won't look at me?"

"And your tongue says nothing now, Jokanaan, your tongue that was like a red snake spitting poison at me? That's strange, isn't it? How is it that the red viper moves no more? You spoke evil words against me, Salome, daughter of Herodias, Princess of Judaea."

"Well then! I am still alive, but you are dead, and your head belongs to me! I'm free to do with it what I will. I can do what I want with it; I can throw it to the dogs and to the birds of the air. The birds of the air will devour what the dogs leave behind."

"Ah! Ah! Jokanaan, Jokanaan, you were beautiful. Your body was a column of ivory set on silver feet. It was a garden full of doves and silver lilies. Nothing in the world was so white as your body. Nothing in the world was as black as your hair. And in the whole world nothing was a red as your mouth."

"Your voice was like a censer that scattered strange perfumes, and when I looked at you I heard strange music. Ah! Why didn't you look at me, Jokanaan? You covered your eyes in order to see your God. Well, you saw your God, Jokanaan, but me, me, you never saw. If you had seen me, you would have loved me!"

"I am thirsting for your beauty. I am hungry for your body. Neither wine nor apples can ease my desire. What shall I do now, Jokanaan? Neither floods nor great waters can ever quench the heat of my strong passion. Oh why didn't you look at me? If you had looked at me you would have loved me. I know well that you would have loved me. I know well that you would have loved me. And the mystery of love is greater than the mystery of death."

Salome remains intoxicated and enraptured, exhausted and brooding as she contemplates the decapitated head of the Prophet. Herod mutters to Herodias: "She is a monster, your daughter." Herodias acknowledges Herod's accusation with pride, sharing her daughter's victory. Now she insists that they remain on the terrace: "I approve of what she did. I'll stay here now." But Herod wants to leave the horrible scene, afraid and fearful, and wanting to hide in the palace because he fears that something terrible will happen.

Herod becomes seized with terror. He commands his slaves: "Put out the torches! Hide the moon, hide the stars!" Suddenly, the moon and stars disappear behind the clouds and it becomes eerily dark. In the dimness of the night, Salome, gripped by her unconscious erotic delirium, continues to lustfully kiss the severed head of Jokanaan.

"Ah! I have kissed your mouth, Jokanaan. There was a bitter taste on your lips. Was it the taste of blood? No, perhaps it is the taste of love. They say that love has a bitter taste. But so what? I have kissed your mouth, Jokanaan. I have now kissed you mouth."

In her final ecstasy of perversity, Salome passes into a strangely mystical sphere of insanity, the climactic fulfillment of her erotic yearnings and desires.

A moonbeam falls on Salome, covering her with light. Before departing, Herod turns to witness Salome, illuminated by the beam of moonlight, intoxicated in her orgasmic and passionate ritual, her insane lust as she kisses the severed head of the prophet.

Disgusted, fearful, and terrified by the horror, Herod commands his Soldiers: "Man töte dieses Welb!" ("Kill that woman!")

The Soldiers crush Princess Salome between their shields.

Commentary and Analysis

Richard Strauss (1864 – 1949) became the foremost post-Wagnerian German Romantic composer during the late nineteenth and twentieth centuries, his fame attributed to his genius as a composer of opera, lieder, or art songs, and symphonic poems. Strauss's musical style was distinctly different from the hyper-Romanticism of his predecessor, Richard Wagner: his musical signature was unique, individual and independent.

Strauss was born and educated in Munich, the son of Franz Strauss, his father recognized at the time as Germany's leading French horn virtuoso. From the age of 4, the young Richard devoted all of his energies to music: by age 18, he had copiously composed more than 140 works that included lieder, chamber works and orchestral pieces. Those early compositions were strongly influenced by his father: they were classical, and rigidly formal in structure.

In 1884, at the age of 20, Strauss was commissioned by Hans von Bülow to compose the *Suite for 13 Winds* for the Meiningen orchestra. He conducted the work's premiere which led to his appointment as assistant conductor of the orchestra. Henceforth, Strauss became eminent as both composer and conductor, conducting major orchestras in both Germany and Austria, and establishing a stunning reputation for his interpretations of Mozart and Wagner. Eventually, he became director of the Royal Court Opera in Berlin (1898-1919), and musical co-director of the Vienna State Opera (1919-1924).

Strauss's musical compositions fall into three distinct periods. His compositions from his first period (1880-87) include a *Sonata for Cello and Piano* (1883), *Burleske* for piano and orchestra (1885), and the symphonic fantasy, *Aus Italien* (1887) ("From Italy"), the latter heavily influenced by the styles of Liszt and Wagner. In his early years, Strauss nurtured his admiration for Wagner in secret so as not to affront the elder Strauss who detested Wagner both musically and personally.

In Strauss's second creative period (1887-1904), he established his unique musical style and signature, in particular, his unprecedented mastery of orchestration. Like Franz Liszt, he abandoned classical forms in order to express his musical ideas in the programmatic symphonic tone poem, an orchestral medium that was totally free from classical strictures and rigid forms. Strauss perfected the tone poem form: he imbued it with profound drama that was achieved through the interweaving and recurrence of leitmotif themes, and the exploitation of the expressive power of a huge orchestra, the latter saturated with impassioned melodiousness, descriptive instrumentation, and harmonic richness. With Strauss, the tone poem form became endowed with a new vision and a new language, innovating harmonies, and instrumentation that greatly expanded the expressive possibilities of the modern symphony orchestra; nevertheless, his textures were always refined, and achieved an almost chamber-music delicacy. Strauss was an Expressionist, seeking to depict through his musical language subjective emotions and subconscious states, all of which were expressed with his highly personal and independent musical signature.

Strauss's symphonic poems dominated his musical output during this second creative period: *Don Juan* (1889), *Macbeth* (1890), *Tod und Verklärung* ("Death and Transfiguration") (1890), *Till Eulenspiegels lustige Streiche* ("Till Eulenspiegel's Merry Pranks") (1895), *Also Sprach Zarathustra* ("Thus Spoke Zarathustra") (1896), *Don Quixote* (1897), and *Ein Heldenleben* ("A Hero's Life") (1898), the latter portraying Strauss himself as the hero, and his critics his adversaries. In 1903, he composed the *Symphonia Domestica* for a huge orchestra, its programmatic theme describing a full day in the Strauss family's household, including duties tending to the children, marital quarrels, and even the intimacy of the bedroom.

Strauss's Expressionism was magnificently demonstrated in works such as *Till Eulenspiegel's Merry Pranks,* its instrumental colors depicting the fourteenth century rogue's adventures that included the sounds of pots and pans, and the hero's murmurs as he goes to the gallows: in *Also Sprach Zarathustra*, ostensibly a homage to Nietzsche, the essences of man and nature are brilliantly contrasted through varying tonalities; and in *Don Quixote*, the music magically captures images of sheep, windmills, and flying horses.

During Strauss's third period (1904-49), he became the foremost opera composer in the world. Earlier, he had composed his first opera, *Guntram* (1894), but it was a failure, considered a slavish imitation of Wagner. His second opera, *Feuersnot* (1902) ("Fire-Famine"), was a satirical comic opera about small town prudery and hypocrisy, also poorly received. Strauss was not yet in full command of his operatic powers.

In 1905, Strauss emerged into operatic greatness with *Salome*, a blasphemous, obscene, explosive, and unprecedented "shocker" portraying female obsessions: *Salome* immediately became a major triumph in all the major opera houses of the world; one notable exception, Vienna, where the powerful prelates forbade Gustav Mahler to stage it. Strauss followed with *Elektra* (1909), his first collaboration with the Austrian poet and dramatist, Hugo von Hofmannsthal: *Elektra* became another exploration of female fixations, in this case revenge.

Both *Salome* and *Elektra* were composed for the opera stage as one continuous scene: one-act operas containing intense and concentrated dramatic action. Strauss, a contemporary of Zola, Ibsen, Wilde, and the fin de siècle malaise, demonstrated in these operas that he was a supreme master of psychological shock, who possessed a deft genius to convey intense emotion through the power of his music: he was a musical dramatist par excellence — as well as a musical psychologist — who was most comfortable with emotionally complex and supercharged characters; Salome, Elektra, and the Marschallin in *Der Rosenkavalier* (1911). Both *Salome* and *Elektra* contain furious explosions of human emotion, pathological passion, perversity, horror, terror, and madness; both operas contain subtexts representing subtle predictions of the psychopathic events that would unfold as the twentieth century progressed.

Hugo von Hofmannsthal eventually exercised a profound influence on Strauss: they collaborated on 6 operas, all of which are considered Strauss's finest works. After *Elektra*, Strauss abandoned the violence and psychological realism of "shock" opera and composed *Der Rosenkavalier*, a "comedy in music" set in eighteenth century Vienna, its story, a sentimental evocation of tenderness, nostalgia, romance, and humor, which is accented by anachronistic yet extremely sentimental waltzes.

Ariadne auf Naxos (1912, revised 1916), conveys the delicacy of Mozart combined with Wagnerian heroism, a play-within-a-play blending commedia dell'arte satire with classical tragedy: the philosophical *Die Frau ohne Schatten* (1919) ("The Woman without a Shadow") is a symbolic and deeply psychological fairy tale in which the spiritual and real worlds collide; *Intermezzo* (1924), the libretto by the composer, is a thinly disguised Strauss with his wife, Pauline, in a domestic comedy involving misunderstandings emanating from a misdirected love letter from an unknown female admirer; *Die Äegyptische Helena* (1928) ("The Egyptian Helen") is based on an episode from Homer's Odyssey; and Strauss's final collaboration with Hofmannsthal, *Arabella* (1933), returns to the ambience of *Der Rosenkavalier's* Vienna and its amorous intrigues and romance.

After Hofmannsthal's death, Strauss composed operas with other librettists, though never equaling his earlier successes: *Die Schweigsame Frau* (1935) ("The Silent Woman"), a delightful comedy written to a libretto by Stefan Zweig after Ben Jonson; *Friedenstag* (1938) ("Peace Day"); *Daphne* (1938); *Midas* (1939); *Die Liebe der Danae* ("The Love of Danae") completed in 1940 but not staged until 1952; and his final opera, *Capriccio* (1942), an opera-about-an-opera described by its authors as "a conversation piece for music," in which the relative importance and balance of opera's text and music is argued.

Strauss was most fertile in producing songs — lieder — some of the finest after those of Schumann and Brahms. Among the most esteemed are: *Zueignung* ("Dedication") (1882-83) and *Morgen* ("Morning") (1893-94). Other works include the ballet *Josephslegende* ("Legend of Joseph") (1914), *Eine Alpensinfonie* ("Alpine Symphony") (1915), and *Vier Letzte Lieder* ("Four Last Songs") (1948).

Strauss's musical style was daring, brilliant, ornate, and ostentatious; a post-Romantic bravura that thoroughly pleased audiences during the late nineteenth and early twentieth centuries, and continues in contemporary times. Although the successes of *Salome* and *Elektra* earned him accolades as an avant-garde composer, after *Der Rosenkavalier,* which followed *Elektra,* he became more conservative and classical, unaffected by experiments in serial and atonal music or the harmonic adventurism that was dominating his contemporary musical world. The greater part of his career ——— the 38 years following *Der Rosenkavalier*—- was spent polishing his unique style, striving for a perfect fusion between the distinctive refinement and delicacy of Mozart, and the profound poetic and dramatic expressiveness of the Romantics.

Strauss remained in Nazi Germany during the entire Second World War, which in hindsight has cast doubts on his humanity and personal integrity. But in fact, Strauss was neither interested nor skilled in politics, and no one of his operas — before or after the Nazis — contains a political subtext or underlying ideological message. In 1933, after the National Socialists came into power, Strauss at first identified closely with the new regime, unwittingly allowing him to be used as an instrument of their propaganda machinery. Although he served as president of the Reichsmusikkammer, the state's Chamber of Music, from 1933 to 1935, it was very soon thereafter that he came into conflict with government officials; in particular, after his association with the dramatist, Stefan Zweig.

After Hofmannsthal's death in 1929, Strauss collaborated with the Jewish dramatist Stefan Zweig on the lighthearted comedy *Die Schweigsame Frau* ("The Silent Woman"), a relationship with a Jewish artist that became unacceptable and particularly embarrassing — if not scandalous — to the Nazis; that association with Zweig as librettist for an opera was contrary to every stricture by which good Nazis lived, and at the time, violated Nazi laws promulgated against Jews. But for the Nazis to prohibit an opera written by Richard Strauss, at that time the most revered German composer in the world, was to invite a storm of international protest.

Nevertheless, the Nazis eliminated Zweig's name as librettist for the opera and cited the story as an adaptation "From the English of Ben Johnson"; in protest and defiance, Strauss restored Zweig's name to the libretto with his own hand. After the premiere of *Die Schweigsame Frau* in 1935, the opera was banned after 4 performances: Strauss was forced to resign as president of the Chamber of Music and he was compelled to work with a non-Jewish librettist: Joseph Gregor.

But above all else, Strauss was a family man, who was forced to use every iota of his influence as Germany's greatest living composer to protect his Jewish daughter-in-law, Alice Grab, and his two grandchildren. Earlier, at the wedding of his son Franz, it had been quipped that the event heralded the funeral of the virulent anti-Semitism he presumably inherited from his father. But somewhere along the line, for practical purposes, Strauss seemingly collaborated with the Nazis and made an arrangement: he would not speak out against the Nazis, but they in turn would not harm his daughter-in-law and two grandchildren.

In his defense, Strauss claimed to be apolitical: art supersedes politics. He tried to ignore his perception of the Nazi's disgrace to German honor, but in the early phases of the Nazi regime he did become the compliant artist who quickly usurped the music posts of emigrating Jewish artists, such as Bruno Walter. In 1933, after Toscanini withdrew from a *Parsifal* performance at Bayreuth in protest, he later met Strauss in Milan and greeted him with a stinging remark: "As a musician I take my hat off to you. As a man I put it on again." Nevertheless, Toscanini was not living in Nazi Germany, nor did he have to protect a Jewish daughter-in-law or Jewish grandchildren.

Life under the Nazis could not have been pleasant for Strauss, but he was too important to be treated harshly. In effect, Strauss was tolerated by the government, regarded with suspicion, but treated with contempt. At one point, a hysterical propaganda minister, Goebbels, forced him to relinquish his cherished Garmisch villa and make it available for bomb victims.

Strauss spent part of World War II out of the limelight: in Vienna, and later in Switzerland. After the war, he was investigated by an allied commission which exonerated him of any collaboration with the Nazis. Strauss was no hero, nor was he a martyr. In historical hindsight, it would be presumptuous and unjust to stand in judgment of Strauss's politics. In the aftermath of the horror of the Second World War, Strauss was another suffering artist, struggling for survival in a world that went mad: nevertheless, his less than heroic opposition to the Third Reich continues to shade perceptions of his works and his character. In 1949, Strauss returned to Garmisch where he died three months after his 85th birthday.

Herod was the name of several Roman-appointed rulers in ancient Palestine during the first century: they were Idumaeans, or Edomites, descendants of the biblical Esau who lived in the geographic area of Idumaea that lies south of Judaea and the Dead Sea.

Herod the Great — "Great" because he was an eldest son — was prized by the Romans for his intense loyalty, his unusual abilities as a ruthless fighter, and his subtle diplomacy, but more importantly, for his ability to subdue opposition and maintain order and control in the volatile province of Palestine. Under Herod the Great's rule, Palestine experienced economic and cultural growth: many important buildings were erected, including his greatest achievement, the rebuilding of the Temple in Jerusalem; he was also in the vanguard to introduce Hellenistic (Greek) ideas and culture into Palestine.

Jesus was born in Bethlehem during the reign of Herod the Great. The Gospel relates that Herod the Great attempted to suppress the Messianic calling by ordering all male infants in Bethlehem slain: according to the Gospel of Matthew, Joseph and Mary had a dream in which they were alerted by God to flee to Egypt with their child and hide there until Herod's death.

Herod Antipas, 21 BC – AD 39 — the Herod in the *Salome* story — was the son of Herod the Great. He was appointed tetrarch, or Roman governor, ruling Galilee and Perea from 4 BC to 39 AD, the major part of Jesus' life and ministry.

The story about Salome, and the historical events involving her stepfather Herod Antipas, her mother Herodias, and the beheading of John the Baptist, is told in the Gospels of Mark (6:14-29) and Matthew (14:1-12). The story is also mentioned by Flavius Josephus, an ancient Jewish historian whose *Antiquitates Judaicae* ("The Antiquities of the Jews"), is a chronicle of Jewish history during the first century BC through the great revolt of 66-70 AD. The actual historic truth about Salome beyond those sources remains obscure, supplemented over the course of two thousand years by legend and fiction.

The story of Salome is recounted in the Gospel, Mark 6:14-29:

14   King Herod heard about this, for Jesus' name had become well known. Some were saying, "John the Baptist has been raised from the dead, and that is why miraculous powers are at work in him."

15   Others said, "He is Elijah." And still others claimed, "He is a prophet, like one of the prophets of long ago."

16   But when Herod heard this, he said, "John, the man I beheaded, has been raised from the dead!"

17   For Herod himself had given orders to have John arrested, and he had him bound and put in prison. He did this because of Herodias, his brother Philip's wife, whom he had married.

18   For John had been saying to Herod, "It is not lawful for you to have your brother's wife."

19   So Herodias nursed a grudge against John and wanted to kill him. But she was not able to,

20   because Herod feared John and protected him, knowing him to be a righteous and holy man. When Herod heard John, he was greatly puzzled; yet he liked to listen to him.

21   Finally the opportune time came. On his birthday Herod gave a banquet for his high officials and military commanders and the leading men of Galilee.

22   When the daughter of Herodias came in and danced, she pleased Herod and his dinner guests. The king said to the girl, "Ask me for anything you want, and I'll give it to you."

23   And he promised her with an oath, "Whatever you ask I will give you, up to half my kingdom."

24   She went out and said to her mother, "What shall I ask for?" "The head of John the Baptist," she answered.

25   At once the girl hurried in to the king with the request: "I want you to give me right now the head of John the Baptist on a platter."

26   The king was greatly distressed, but because of his oaths and his dinner guests, he did not want to refuse her.

27   So he immediately sent an executioner with orders to bring John's head. The man went, beheaded John in the prison,

28   and brought back his head on a platter. He presented it to the girl, and she gave it to her mother.

29   On hearing of this, John's disciples came and took his body and laid it in a tomb.

And the Salome story is also recounted in the Gospel of Matthew 14:1-12:

1   At that time Herod the tetrarch heard the reports about Jesus,

2   and he said to his attendants, "This is John the Baptist; he has risen from the dead! That is why miraculous powers are at work in him."

3   Now Herod had arrested John and bound him and put him in prison because of Herodias, his brother Philip's wife,

4   for John had been saying to him: "It is not lawful for you to have her."

5   Herod wanted to kill John, but he was afraid of the people, because they considered him a prophet.

6   On Herod's birthday the daughter of Herodias danced for them and pleased Herod so much

7   that he promised with an oath to give her whatever she asked.

8   Prompted by her mother, she said, "Give me here on a platter the head of John the Baptist."

9   The king was distressed, but because of his oaths and his dinner guests, he ordered that her request be granted

10   and had John beheaded in the prison.

11   His head was brought in on a platter and given to the girl, who carried it to her mother.

12   John's disciples came and took his body and buried it. Then they went and told Jesus.

All accounts agree that Herod became infatuated with Herodias, the wife of his half-brother, Philip. One legend claims that Herod killed his half-brother, eloping with Herodias after he also killed his wife, Marianne, a brutal murder that haunted him throughout his reign.

Another less sinister legend claims that he merely divorced his wife in order to marry Herodias. Nonetheless, both versions of the Gospel relate that the evangelical preacher, John the Baptist, condemned Herod's marriage to Herodias because divorce was a violation of Mosaic law. Infuriated by the Prophet's denunciation of her, Herodias goaded Herod to imprison John; however, Herod did not condemn the popular Prophet to death, fearing it would instigate unrest from among the masses. Infuriated, Herodias inveigled her daughter, Salome, to demand the Baptist's head as her reward for dancing for her stepfather at his birthday celebration. As such, the Gospel accounts place the responsibility for John's execution on Herodias rather than Salome. So in the Gospels, it is Herodias who engineers the prophet's death; her motive, revenge for John's audacious condemnation of her marriage to Herod. The reluctant Herod was bound by oath to have John beheaded, and it was Herodias's daughter, Salome, who presented the platter with John's decapitated head to her vengeful and victorious mother.

But in the Gospels there is no mention of Salome by name; she is simply referred to as the "daughter of Herodias." And there is also no specific mention of the "Dance of the Seven Veils" in the Gospels, but merely a general reference to a dance that Salome performed for Herod.

Ironically, the name Salome means peace. In the New Testament, the only Salome mentioned by name is one of the women who witnessed the crucifixion of Jesus, and who later brought spices to the tomb to anoint His body; she was apparently the mother of James and John, two disciples of Jesus; and she is depicted in the Gospel of Matthew asking special favors for her sons.

Flavius Josephus attributes John's execution to neither Salome nor Herodias: according to Josephus, the Prophet was not imprisoned or executed for his outspoken denunciation of Herod's marriage to Herodias, but was executed by Herod for political reasons, the Tetrarch motivated by his fear of John's power to incite religious rebellion and revolt.

John the Baptist was a moral reformer and preacher of the Messianic Deliverance. The Gospels relate that Herod arrested and imprisoned him because he feared that his outspoken evangelical exhortations of repentance and salvation would foment unrest in his province, an irritation to their Roman conquerors.

The Gospels are unanimous in their description that John lived in the wilderness where he received his sacred calling, preaching there until his arrest and execution. In Biblical times, the wilderness, a vast wasteland of crags, wind, and heat, was a place where the ancients believed God had dwelled with His people after the Exodus; it was a place that represented spiritual hope for the people of Israel. With resolve and urgency, John called people from the comforts of their homes into the wilderness where they were to meet God and repent for their sins: he challenged them to share clothing and food, and criticized them for their presumptuousness and their sense of righteousness merely because they were descendants of Abraham. John drew large crowds who heard him preach moral reform in preparation for the Messianic Deliverance, invoking renewal through baptism, the symbol moral regeneration.

Ultimately, Herod Antipas was involved in Jesus' trial. After Jesus was arrested in Jerusalem, Pilate, the Roman procurator in Judaea, first sent Jesus to Herod because He was a subject in his region. Herod returned Jesus to Pilate, unable to find anything substantive in the charges that deserved death, and he was therefore unwilling to pass judgment.

After Herod Antipas' death, Palestine struggled through a number of chaotic years, culminating in the revolt of 70 AD in which Rome would finally establish order in the region by dispersing the Jews from the land.

Oscar Wilde became inspired to the Salome subject most probably through the renowned paintings by Gustave Moreau, for whom the story had long been an obsessive fascination: Salome had also been the subject of painters for centuries; Rubens, Durer, Stanzoni, Titian, and Aubrey Beardsley. Wilde was also no doubt familiar with Huysmans' novel, *À Rebours* (1884), Flaubert's *Hérodias* (1877), as well the works of the German lyric poet, Heinrich Heine. In Flaubert's version, upon which Massenet's opera *Hérodiade* (1881) is based, John the Baptist is in love with Salome. When the jealous Herod kills John, Salome stabs herself. And in some medieval legends, Herodias herself was in love with the Baptist.

Wilde published *Salome* in 1893. It began as a prose narrative, was transformed into a poem, and then into a play, the latter written in French for the renowned actress, Sara Bernhardt, although she never performed it. Even though Wilde was equally at home in French as well as English, its original writing in French was unable to protect it from being condemned as an audacious work; the play got as far as a rehearsal in London, but almost immediately its license was refused by the Lord Chamberlain's office. Up until 1931, the play was banned in England as an "arrangement of blood and ferocity, morbid, bizarre, and repulsive." The German version, translated by Hedwig Lachmann, was first performed in Germany in 1901, and one year later, was produced by Max Reinhardt at his Kleines Theater in Berlin, where it had a remarkable run of some 200 performances.

In Wilde's play, Salome drives the central dramatic action. Wilde added his own luster to the original story sources by presenting the drama with a profound collision of Christian and pagan values. But in Wilde's version, it is Salome, rather than her mother Herodias, who is the instigator of the Prophet's execution; she plays cunningly with Herod's crazed passion for her, and is even undeterred by Herodias's attempts to dissuade her. Salome's dance earned her a reward from Herod which becomes the instrument that leads to the Prophet's death.

Wilde's version of the story transcended the few lines narrated in the Gospels: he commented that his purpose was to write a play "About a woman dancing with her bare feet in the blood of a man she craved for and had slain." His focus was to expose recurring motifs of doom, the obsessions of gender power, and the unconscious erotic desires that lead to horrifying evil. Therefore, Wilde's Salome portrays the sexual obsession and lust of a teenage young virgin: he depicts her as evil incarnate, and nothing, he claimed, can be as evil as the innocent erotic desires that are evoked from her unconscious.

Wilde intentionally wanted his Salome to be scandalous, an outrageous manifestation of unconscious, relentless lust, a perversion approaching sadism, or, the conflict inherent in the feminine desire for sexual power over men. Ultimately, Wilde created his demon: Salome is a monstrous beast, like the Helen of ancient myth, who becomes indifferent, irresponsible, insensible, and poisonous to everything she touches; Wilde's Salome becomes consumed and possessed by infinite perversity.

Wilde — and later Strauss — were considered madmen, the creators of a neo-pagan version of the New Testament story that was deemed brutal, shocking, and neurotic: it was deliberately "morbid," "perverse," and "immoral," the critics unable to distinguish between art and life, as well as between illusion and reality.

Nevertheless, artistic intuition usually transcends man's ordinary consciousness: in *The Bacchae* of Euripides, the female mind was portrayed as prone to hysteria and a perversity of sexual passion while it escaped from the restraints imposed by social convention. Likewise, in *Salome,* Wilde was anticipating some of the mysterious and somber discoveries of the psychiatrists. In *The Critic as Artist* (1890), Wilde addressed human motivation and proclaimed that it was "the liberty of the modern artist to probe the darkest and socially more distasteful recesses of the human mind," and, "there is still much to be done in the sphere of introspection." He added, "People sometimes say that fiction is getting too morbid. We have merely touched the surface of the soul, that is all. In one single ivory cell of the brain there are stored away things more marvelous and more terrible than even they have dreamed of who, like the author of *Le Rouge et Le Noir*, have sought to track the soul into its most secret places, and to make life confess its dearest sins." (*Le Rouge et Le Noir* ("The Red and the Black") refers to Stendhal's novel depicting an unsentimental and relentless opportunist who employs seduction as a means to advancement.)

In 1901, a production of Wilde's *Salome* reached many German towns. It attracted Strauss's attention and he soon commented that the play "cried out for music," considering Wilde's repetition or recurrence of "motifs" to be dramatic elements that seemed to naturally adapt to musical scoring.

The Viennese poet, Anton Linder, sent Strauss a proposed libretto, but the composer was uncomfortable with it, failing to be either impressed or inspired by it. However, Strauss had read and seen the Berlin production of *Salome* that was based on Hedwig Lachmann German translation — with Gertrud Eysoldt in the title role — and realized that it was inherently far superior to a conventional opera libretto, particularly that of Linder. One day an idea struck him: "Why not set Wilde's (prose) text very much as it stands?", Strauss recalling how he had become mesmerized by the musical possibilities of the play's very first line: "Wie schön ist die Prinzessin Salome, heute Nacht!" ("How beautiful the Princess Salome is tonight!")

Strauss was determined to be faithful to Lachmann's translation. Nevertheless, some excisions had to be made, practical and necessary condensations of the text that become obligatory when spoken drama is transformed into musical drama. Those cuts involved removing some of Wilde's poetic intensity and expansive and luxuriant verbal imagery, elements Strauss was able to replace with the grandeur of his musical language.

In Wilde's opening scene, the Page attempts to bring reason into the Salome-infatuated mind of the young Narraboth, the Syrian Captain of the Guard. Strauss minimizes the Narraboth-Page interchange, keeping the subplot ostensibly in the background because it would have added an element of lament and poignancy that would interfere with the opera's primary dramatic thrust: Salome's obsession with the Prophet. In Wilde, after Narraboth's suicide, the Page expresses a passionate lament for his dead friend: Strauss likewise omitted that scene, among his other reasons, that it would have required another leading singer.

Similarly, in Wilde's opening scene, the Nubian and Cappadocian soldiers discuss religion: the Nubian comments about his people's holy sacrifices and their lust for blood; the Cappadocian fears that the Romans have driven his country's gods into oblivion. Later, both soldiers comment about the Jews who worship a God and believe in thing they cannot see. Strauss omits this discussion, resuming the continuous fury and frenzy of the drama with Jokanaan's annunciation from the cistern, followed by the Page's despairing appeal to Narraboth: "You're always looking at her. You look at her too much. It's dangerous to look at people in such a way. Something terrible will happen."

Strauss also made certain excisions from Wilde's play that are significantly relevant to the story. As an example, in the opening scene, a soldier tells a Cappadocian that the Prophet came from the wilderness, and that his utterances are often difficult to understand. The Cappadocian points to the cistern and comments that it is a strange prison, old, and certainly unhealthy. The Second Soldier intervenes to reveal that the Tetrarch's older brother (Philip), the king who was the first husband of Herodias, was imprisoned there for twelve years. Philip's incarceration in the cistern did not kill him, so at the end of the twelve years he had to be strangled. The Cappadocian reacts in horror. The Soldier points to the executioner, Naaman, a huge Negro, who was the Executioner who strangled the Tetrarch's brother. And the Soldier further advises him that Naaman had no fear, because the Tetrarch sent him the death-ring. And, Salome certainly reacted with subconscious horror when she first saw the cistern, the prison her own father was condemned to by her stepfather Herod. These elements have a profound bearing on the later development of the plot.

In sum, about one third of Wilde's play was omitted from Strauss's *Salome*. Nevertheless, Strauss was religiously faithful to every word of Wilde's prose in the long final scene: Salome's apostrophe to the decapitated head of the Prophet.

Wilde's play provided Strauss with an organic unity, a balance of tension, relaxation and climax. Strauss builds three gradual ascents to a climax, a gradual crescendo of horror in which a present scene makes a more dramatic impact than the previous scene. The first major scene involves Salome's awakening, her enunciation of her morbid passion and desire for the Prophet; it is in this first scene that the music associated with the head of the Baptist is first heard: a Richard Strauss waltz. The second scene involves the collision between the Prophet and Salome, her obsession with the beauty of his body, and his rejection and denunciation of her as the daughter of the iniquitous Herodias. At the end of this scene, Narraboth commits suicide, and shortly thereafter, Jokanaan descends into the cistern, the scene culminating in a thunderous collision of themes associated with Salome and the Prophet. The third scene involves Salome's cunningly engineered dance to the crashing of her last link with sanity; in the final moments, her passions explode over the decapitated head of the Prophet.

A fter Salome entered rehearsals in Dresden, inherent problems with the opera erupted. In particular, singer after singer declared his or her part unsingable and wished to withdraw. The Salome, the dramatic soprano, Frau Wittich, went on strike; she became shocked by the strenuousness of the role; it was a role written for a sixteen-year-old princess with the voice of Isolde, whose voice had to override a massive orchestra. She cried out to Strauss in consternation: "One just does not write like that, Herr Strauss; either one thing or the other." And then she proclaimed her righteous indignation in performing the disgraceful lead role: "That I won't do; I am a respectable woman." But Frau Wittich conceded, for Salome was too lush a singing role to refuse, even though she found the role difficult to learn.

Aside from all of its rehearsal difficulties, the opera premiered on December 9, 1905, the musical pundits arrogantly confident that the opera would have a short life because of its demands for such a large orchestra, and its requirement for so many rehearsals. Their *Schadenfreude,* as well as their vociferous puritanical outrage was short-lived: in spite of its controversy, *Salome* quickly established itself in German opera houses, and later internationally. The clergy voiced their denunciations as late as 1918, causing a proposed production at the Vienna Staatsoper to be abandoned because of the intervention of the influential Austrian prelate, appropriately named Archbishop Piffl. In 1939, the opera was banned in Austria, condemned as a "Jewish ballad."

In 1910, Salome was finally performed in England, where earlier the Lord Chamberlain had forbidden performances of Wilde's play. This time, it was demanded that biblical references be deleted: John the Baptist became a prophet named Mattaniah, the action was moved from Judaea to Greece, and the Jews and Nazarenes became "Learned Men" and "Cappadocians." Of course, there was no head of the Baptist in the final scene, the young princess pouring out her climactic passions to a dish of blood.

W ilde commented that Salome's recurring prose motifs accommodated music: it is "like a piece of music," and that he had "bound it together as a ballad"; his insistent repetitions of key dramatic phrases were indeed the equivalent of musical leitmotifs.

The lowering full moon is a silent participant presiding over the action of the drama, acting as a spotlight that metaphorically and symbolically reflects the underlying tensions of each scene; its alternating light and dark hues reflect the varying mental states and attitudes of each character, their unconscious yearnings, and neurotic fears. Salome herself is like Wilde's poetic symbol of the ambivalent moon; the light it casts, not bright or clear, but dim and mysterious. In that sense, the moon portrays obsessions, ambiguities, weaknesses, and fatal flaws; it is a metaphor of each character.

During the play — and the opera — the moon continuously changes its different faces and hues, alternating from pale, bright, black, and red. In its bright appearance at the very beginning of the opera, Salome refers to the moon as "a silver flower, cool and chaste, with the loveliness of a virgin who has remained pure." Later, the besotted Herod views the moon "like a drunken woman, reeling through the clouds, looking for lovers." The sober, imperturbable, no-nonsense queen Herodias, steeped in vice and impervious to omens, remains more blunt and unmoved by the moon: "No, the moon is like the moon, that is all."

In contrast, the exalted Prophet Jokanaan, whose spirit dwells in the contemplation of the sunshine of religious truth, is untouched by the nocturnal moonlight.

S trauss endowed the *Salome* score with the full force of his Expressionistic musical ideas, his music an invitation to feel rather than just think about its neurotic sensuality, and the twisted and distorted manifestations within the heroine's soul. Strauss's music is both alluring as well as repulsive: in each successive climax, he relentlessly achieves pathological effects by deploying his musico-dramatic genius through harmonic and orchestral explosions that emphasize the psychological aspects of drama. In *Salome,* Strauss's orchestral resources are monstrously overweighted, and aside from the monstrous vocal demands he makes on the principal singer, she must also dance the *Dance of the Seven Veils,* a moment when most intelligent directors perceptively use a stand-in.

Strauss's musical language presents *Salome's* key themes in different disguises. Salome's first theme appears in the disguise of a Viennese waltz, but when it reappears in the final scene, it is saturated with shattering dissonance, a portrait of the grotesque transformation and dysfunction of Salome's mind. Salome's second theme reappears savagely when the severed head is lifted from the cistern, when a cloud obscures the moon, and when Salome kisses the decapitated Prophet.

Salome is without doubt, probably the most extraordinary opera subject ever chosen by a composer: Herod is consumed with lust for his own stepdaughter, who also happens to be his niece; and Salome, an ingénue and innocent, develops a compulsive desire for the religious ascetic, John the Baptist, but when she is thwarted in her erotic desires, she moves heaven and earth to have the man decapitated so she can fulfill her longings, expressed in the most grotesque and perverted form; kissing the lips of the Prophet's severed head.

It is no wonder that at its premiere, Strauss's *Salome* was considered perverse, nerve-racking, monstrous, and even scandalous. The music, far from softening the morbidity of the subject, magnifies and underscores every lurid detail, Strauss clothing its gruesome depravity with every shimmering hue available on the palette of the modern hundred-piece plus orchestra.

Strauss creates sheer nervous tension as he progresses from horror to horror, the expectation of impending doom and depravity pervading the atmosphere from the moment the curtain rises. The music continues to alternate in texture: in one moment, nerves are jangled with strident and terrifying dissonance; in the next, they are lulled into security by mellifluous harmonies; and suddenly, they reverse, striking again with new tonal clashes.

Strauss blends and fuses harmonic styles, providing an enormous contrast — a chiaroscuro — that provides a musical portrait of his characters: the inspired prophet's music, particularly when he prophesies the Messianic Deliverance, is firm, grave, and solemn; the lascivious Herod's music is unstable, neurotic, and shifting; and Salome's final monologue, is a masterpiece of tension and drama, like a symphonic poem with a vocal solo.

The "Dance of the Seven Veils" is perhaps the most famous striptease of all time. In the "Dance," Salome discards the veils one by one, until, at the end, she is supposedly naked, an anomaly for the stout prima donna. A svelte singer may be able to handle the "Dance," but in many performances, it is deputized appropriately to a ballerina.

In both the play and the opera's libretto, Salome removes only her sandals before putting on the veils to dance: Herod derives sensual gratification from the sight of her feet. In Wilde's play, Herod comments, "Ah, you're going to dance with naked feet. 'T'is well. Your little feet will be like white doves. They will be like little white flowers that dance upon the trees."

Musically, the "Dance" is a virtual potpourri of already familiar themes. Nevertheless, after a quasi-oriental beginning, Salome's sensual oriental dance, for the most part, possesses a thoroughly Viennese flavor.

Today, for the most part, people respond to the *Salome* story as a work of art rather than a scandalized story: musical senses have become more attuned to the idioms that Richard Strauss anticipated and matured with, and his style is more objectively appreciated. In essence, the horrors and neuroticisms of the *Salome* story fall into the background before the unrivaled beauty of Strauss's musical language. As in any great work of art, lurid details can be submerged in a flood of the magnificence of the work: *Salome* fuses horror with essential beauty, forcing one to quote Narraboth in the opera: "Wie schön ist die Prinzessin Salome heute Abend!" ("How beautiful Princess Salome is tonight!")

Nevertheless, depravity and decadence were the key words that dominated early descriptions of *Salome*. At its New York premiere, the New York Times complained that *Salome* was a "detailed and explicit exposition of the most horrible, disgusting, revolting and unmentionable features of degeneracy ever heard, read of, or imagined." Other reviews spoke of "smarting eyeballs and wrecked nerves," and that decent men did not want to have their house polluted with the stench with which Oscar Wilde's play had filled the nostrils of humanity. The audience was disgusted yet fascinated: women and men spoke of *Salome* as if they had a bad dream.

The Archbishop of Vienna considered it depraved and tried to have it banned. Likewise, the Kaiser told Strauss: "This will be your ruin." The outraged Metropolitan Opera board of directors considered it so decadent that it was withdrawn after a single performance. The self-proclaimed high priestess of Bayreuth, Cosima Wagner, considered the work "sheer lunacy." Strauss's father, who died just three weeks before his son completed the score, did not like what he had seen thus far: "Oh, God, what nervous music. It is like having your trousers full of maybugs." Gustav Mahler considered it "…a live volcano, a subterranean fire." Others were duly outraged, commenting that it possessed "shock appeal, its libretto a compound of lust, stifling perfumes and blood," and, "cannot be read by any woman or fully understood by anyone but a physician."

Nevertheless, *Salome* represents the culmination of a long battle waged by the late Romanticists in seeking a new kind of artistic truth: the freedom to portray the beauty as well as the ugliness in human experience. In effect, there is beauty in ugliness, by implication, a way in which to achieve inner understanding by experiencing ugliness and evil.

Wilde commented: "People say that fiction is getting too morbid, but as far as psychology is concerned, it has never been morbid enough. We have merely touched the surface of the soul, that is all." In its portraits of the terrible depths of evil, art can provide a moral vision, not the moral vision of the self-righteous man, complacent in the conviction of his own goodness, but the moral vision of the human being made suddenly conscious of his potential for evil, as well as the good in his nature.

Salome still retains the power to shock, its effect an Aristotelian catharsis prompting pity and fear. Salome, a young girl tragically confused by the first stirrings of sexual desire, sees the moon as a chaste virginal flower, but nevertheless, her innocence is haunted by the repressed memory of her father who was imprisoned and killed in the same cistern as John the Baptist. In the sense of catharsis, one senses not revulsion, but a great torrent of cleansing emotion.

Salome brought Freudian psychology to the operatic stage. In the end, Oscar Wilde would have been pleased.

Salome Libretto

A large terrace outside the banquet hall of Herod's palace. It is night, and the moon is full. In the background, there is an old cistern, covered with bronze.
Herodias's young Page and a group of Soldiers lean against a balcony. Narraboth, the young, handsome Syrian Captain of the Guard, looks into the banquet hall.

Allegro

Allegro

NARRABOTH

Wie   schön   ist die Prinzessin Sa - lo - me   heu - te Abend!

Narraboth:
Wie schön ist die Prinzessin Salome
heute Nacht!

Narraboth: *(longingly)*
How beautiful Princess Salome is
tonight!

Page:
Sieh' die Mondscheibe,wie sie seltsam
aussieht.
Wie eine Frau, die aufsteigt aus dem
Grab.

Page:
See how strange the moon looks!

She looks like a woman rising from a
tomb.

Narraboth:
Sie ist sehr seltsam.Wie eine kleine
Prinzessin,
deren Füße weiße Tauben sind.
Man könnte meinen, sie tanzt.

Narraboth:
She has a strange look. She is like a
Princess
who has little white doves as feet.
You would fancy she was dancing.

Page:
Wie eine Frau, die tot ist.
Sie gleitet langsam dahin.

Page:
She's like a pale, dead woman.
She glides along slowly up there.

Erster Soldat:
Was für ein Aufruhr!
Was sind das für wilde Tiere,
die da heulen?

First Soldier: *(reacting to noise)*
What an uproar!
Who are they who are howling like wild
animals?

Zweiter Soldat:
Die Juden. Sie sind immer so.
Sie streiten über ihre Religion.

Second Soldier:
The Jews. They never change.
Always arguing about their religion.

Erster Soldat:
Ich finde es lächerlich,
über solche Dinge zu streiten.

First Soldier:
I think it's ridiculous to dispute about
such matters.

Narraboth:
Wie schön ist die Prinzessin Salome
heute Abend!

Narraboth:
How beautiful Princess Salome is
tonight!

Page:
Du siehst sie immer an.
Du siehst sie zuviel an.
Es ist gefährlich,
Menschen auf diese Art anzusehn.
Schreckliches kann geschehn.

Page: *(anxiously)*
You're always looking at her.
You look at her too much.
It's dangerous to look at people in such
a way.
Something terrible may happen.

Narraboth:
Sie ist sehr schön heute Abend.

Narraboth:
She is very beautiful tonight.

Erster Soldat:
Der Tetrarch sieht finster drein.

First Soldier:
The Tetrarch looks very somber.

Zweiter Soldate:
Ja, er sieht finster drein.

Second Soldier:
Yes, his look is very somber.

Erster Soldate:
Auf wen blickt er?

First Soldier:
Who is he looking at?

Zweiter Soldate:
Ich weiß nicht.

Second Soldier:
I don't know.

Narraboth:
Wie blaß die Prinzessin ist.
Niemals habe ich sie so blaß gesehn.
Sie ist wie der Schatten
eine weißen Rose
in einem silbernen Spiegel.

Narraboth:
How pale the Princess is.
I've never seen her looking so pale.
She's like the shadow
of a rose
reflected in a silver mirror.

Page:
Du mußt sie nicht ansehn.
Du siehst sie zuviel an.
Schreckliches kann geschehn.

Stimme des Jochanaan:
Nach mir wird Einer kommen,
der ist stärker als ich.
Ich bin nicht wert, ihm zu lösen
den Riemen an seinen Schuhn.
Wenn er kommt,
werden die verödeten
Stätten frohlocken.
Wenn er kommt,
werden die Augen der Blinden
den Tag sehn.
Wenn er kommt,
die Ohren der Tauben geöffnet.

Zweiter Soldate:
Heiss' ihn schweigen!

Erster Soldate:
Er ist ein heil'ger Mann.

Zweiter Soldat:
Er sagt immer lächerliche Dinge.

Erster Soldat:
Er ist sehr sanft.
Jeden Tag, den ich ihm zu essen gebe,
dankt er mir.

Ein Cappadocier:
Wer ist es?

Erster Soldat:
Ein Prophet.

Ein Cappadocier:
Wie ist sein Name?

Erster Soldate:
Jochanaan.

Ein Cappadocier:
Woher kommt er?

Page: *(very anxiously)*
You must not look at her.
You look at her too much.
Something terrible may happen.

Voice of Jokanaan:
After me, another shall come,
who is stronger than I.
I am not worthy to undo
the laces of His shoes.
When He comes
all the desolate
places shall rejoice.
When He comes,
the eyes of the blind
shall see the day.
When he comes,
the ears of the deaf shall be opened.

Second Soldier:
Make him be quiet!

First Soldier:
He is a holy man.

Second Soldier:
He's always saying ridiculous things.

First Soldier:
He is very gentle.
Every day when I bring him food,
he thanks me.

A Cappadocian:
Who is he?

First Soldier:
A Prophet.

A Cappadocian:
What's his name?

First Soldier:
Jokanaan.

A Cappadocian:
Where does he come from?

Erster Soldat:
Aus der Wüste.
Eine Schar von Jüngern war dort
immer um ihn.

First Soldier:
From the desert.
A crowd of young people used to flock
to him.

Ein Cappadocier:
Wovon redet er?

A Cappadocian:
What does he talk about?

Erster Soldate:
Unmöglich ist's, zu verstehn,
was er sagt.

First Soldier:
It's impossible to understand
what he says.

Ein Cappadocier:
Kann man ihn sehn?

A Cappadocian:
Can I see him?

Erster Soldate:
Nein, der Tetrarch hat es verboten.

First Soldier:
No, the Tetrarch forbids it.

Narraboth:
Die Prinzessin erhebt sich!
Sie verläßt die Tafel.
Sie ist sehr erregt.
Sie kommt hierher.

Narraboth: *(with excitement)*
The Princess is getting up!
She's leaving the table.
She seems very upset.
She's coming this way.

Page:
Sieh sie nicht an!

Page:
Don't look at her!

Narraboth:
Ja, sie kommt auf uns zu.

Narraboth:
Yes, she's coming towards us.

Page:
Ich bitte dich, sieh sie nicht an!

Page:
I pray to you, don't look at her!

Narraboth:
Sie ist wie eine verirrte Taube.

Narraboth:
She is just like a lost dove.

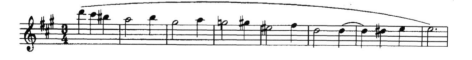

Salome:
Ich will nicht bleiben.
Ich kann nicht bleiben.
Warum sieht mich der Tetrrarch
fortwährend so an mit seinen
Maulwurfsaugen
unter den zuckenden Lidern?

Salome: *(entering excitedly)*
I will not stay there any longer.
I can't stay there any longer.
Why does the Tetrarch
keep looking at me like that
with his mole's eyes
under his shaking eyelids?

Es ist seltsam, daß der Mann
meiner Mutter mich so ansieht.
Wie süß ist hier de Luft!
Hier kann ich atmen.
Da drinnen sitzen Juden
aus Jerusalem, die einander über ihre
närrischen Gebräuche in Stücke reißen.
Schweigsame, list'ge Ägypter
und brutale, ungeschlachte Römer
mit ihrer plumpen Sprache.
O, wie ich diese Römer hasse!

Page:
Schreckliches wird geschehn.
Warum siehst du sie so an?

Salome:
Wie gut ist's, in den Mond zu sehn!
Er ist wie eine silberne Blume,
kühl und keusch.
Ja, wie die Schönheit einer Jungfrau,
die rein geblieben ist.

Stimme des Jochanaan:
Siehe, der Herr ist gekommen,
des Menschen Sohn ist nahe.

Salome:
Wer war das, der hier gerufen hat?

Zweiter Soldat:
Der Prophet, Prinzessin.

Salome:
Ach, der Prophet!
Der, vor dem der Tetrarch Angst hat.

Zweiter Soldat:
Wir wissen davon nichts, Prinzessin.
Es war der Prophet Jochanaan,
der hier rief.

Narraboth:
Beliebt es Euch, daß ich Eure Sänfte
holen lasse, Prinzessin?
Die Nacht ist schön im Garten.

It's odd that my mother's husband
should look at me like that.
How sweet the air is out here!
Here I can breathe freely.
In there sit the Jews
from Jerusalem, tearing at each other
to pieces over all their foolish rituals.
Crafty, quiet Egyptians,
and those brutal and barbarian Romans
with their uncouth language.
Oh, how I loathe the Romans!

Page: *(to Narraboth)*
Something terrible will happen.
Why do you look at her like that?

Salome:
How good it is to see the moon!
She is like a silver flower,
cold and chaste.
Yes, there is a youthful beauty about the
moon, a virgin's beauty.

Voice of Jokanaan:
Behold, the Lord has come,
the Son of Man has come.

Salome:
Who was that, who just spoke?

Second Soldier:
The Prophet, Princess.

Salome:
Ah, the Prophet,
of whom the Tetrarch is so frightened.

Second Soldier:
We know nothing about that, Princess.
It was the Prophet Jokanaan who called
out.

Narraboth: *(to Salome)*
Is it you pleasure that I bid them bring
your couch, my Princess?
The garden is beautiful at night.

Salome:
Er sagt schreckliche Dinge
über meine Mutter, nicht wahr?

Salome:
He says terrible things
about my mother, doesn't he?

Zweiter Soldat:
Wir verstehen nie, was er sagt,
Prinzessin.

Second Soldier:
We don't understand what he says,
Princess.

Salome:
Ja, er sagt schreckliche Dinge über sie.

Salome:
Yes, he says terrible things about her.

Ein Sklave:
Prinzessin, der Tetrarch ersucht Euch,
wieder zum Fest hinein zu gehn.

A Slave:
Princess, the Tetrarch would like you to
return to the feast.

Salome:
Ich will nicht hinein gehn.

Ist dieser Prophet ein alter Mann?

Salome:
I don't want to go back inside.
(to Narraboth)
Is this Prophet an old man?

Narraboth:
Prinzessin, es wäre besser hinein zu
gehn. Gestattet daß ich Euch führe.

Narraboth:
Princess, it will be better if you go
inside. Let me bring you inside.

Salome:
Ist dieser Prophet ein alter Mann?

Salome: *(emphatically)*
Is this Prophet an old man?

Erster Soldat:
Nein, Prinzessin, er ist ganz jung.

First Soldier:
No, Princess, he is quite young.

Stimme des Jochanaan:
Jauchze nicht, du Land Palästina,
weil der Stab dessen,
der dich schlug,
gebrochen ist.
Denn aus dem Samen der Schlange
wird ein Basilisk kommen,
und seine Brut wird die Vögel verschlinge.

Voice of Jokanaan:
Do not rejoice, land of Palestine,
just because the rod of the one
who scourged you
is broken.
For a basilisk shall come
from the seed of the serpent;
its offspring shall devour the birds.

Salome:
Welch seltsame Stimme!
Ich möchte mit ihm sprechen.

Salome:
What a strange voice!
I would like to speak to him.

Zweiter Soldat:
Prinzessin, der Tetrarch duldet nicht,
daß irgend wer mit ihm spricht.

Second Soldier:
Princess, the Tetrarch doesn't want
anyone to speak to him.

Er hat selbst dem Hohenpriester
verboten, mit ihm zu sprechen.

Salome:
Ich wünsche mit ihm zu sprechen.

Zweiter Soldat:
Es ist unmöglich, Prinzessin.

Salome:
Ich will mit ihm sprechen.
Bringt diesen Propheten heraus!

Zweiter Soldat:
Wir dürfen nicht, Prinzessin.

Salome:
Wie schwarz es da drunten ist!
Es muß schrecklich sein, in so einer
schwarzen Höhle zu leben.
Es ist wie eine Gruft.

Habt ihr nicht gehört?
Bringt den Propheten heraus!
Ich möchte ihn sehn!

Erster Soldat:
Prinzessin, wir dürfen nicht tun,
was ihr von uns begehrt.

Salome:
Ah!

Page:
O, was wird geschehn?
Ich weiß, es wird Schreckliches
geschehn.

Salome:
Du wirst das für mich tun,
Narraboth, nicht wahr?
Ich war dir immer gewogen.
Du wirst das für mich tun.
Ich möchte ihn blos sehn,
diesen seltsamen Propheten.
Die Leute haben soviel
von ihm gesprochen.

He has forbidden even the High Priest
to speak to him.

Salome:
I wish to speak to him now.

Second Soldier:
It's not possible, Princess.

Salome:
I want to speak to him.
Have this Prophet brought out!

Second Soldier:
We're not allowed to, Princess.

Salome: *(looking down into the cistern)*
How dark it is down there!
It must be terrible, to live in such a
black pit.
It's just like a tomb.
(to the Soldiers)
Didn't you hear what I said?
Bring the Prophet out!
I want to see him!

First Soldier:
Princess, we can't do what you have
asked of us.

Salome: *(looking to Narraboth)*
Ah!

Page:
Oh, what will happen now?
I'm sure it will be something terrible.

Salome: *(to Narraboth)*
You will do this for me, Narraboth,
won't you?
I've always been kind to you.
You will do this for me.
I just want to see,
this strange Prophet.
People have talked
about him so much.

Ich glaube, der Tetrarch hat Angst vor ihm.

I think the Tetrarch is afraid of him.

Narraboth:
Der Tetrarch hat es ausdrücklich verboten,daß irgend wer den Deckel zu diesem Brunnen aufhebt.

Narraboth:
The Tetrarch has forbidden anyone to raise the cover of the cistern.

.

Salome:
Du wirst das für mich tun,
Narraboth, und morgen,
wenn ich in einer Sänfte
an dem Torweg,
wo die Götzenbilder stehn,
vorbeikomme,
werde ich eine kleine Blume
für dich fallen lassen,
ein kleines grünes Blümchen.

Salome:
You will do this for me,
Narraboth, and tomorrow,
when I pass through the gateway
in my litter
where the idol-makers stand,
when I see you,
I shall drop
a little flower for you.
A little green flower.

Narraboth:
Prinzessin, ich kann nicht, ich kann nicht.

Narraboth:
Princess, I cannot, I cannot!

Salome:
Du wirst das für mich tun, Narraboth.
Du weißt, daß du das für mich tun wirst.
Und morgen früh werde ich
unter denn Muss'linschleiern
dir einen Blick zuwerfen,
Narraboth,
ich werde dich ansehn, kann sein,
ich werde dir zulächeln.

Salome: *(more assertively)*
You'll do this for me, Narraboth.
You know that you will do this for me.
And tomorrow morning,
when I glance at you through my veil,
I shall look at you,
Narraboth,
I shall look at you, and perhaps,
even give you a smile.

Sieh mich an, Narraboth,
sieh mich an.
Ah! Wie gut du weißt,
daß du tun wirst,
um was ich dich bitte.
Wie du es weißt.
Ich weiß, du wirst das tun.

Look at me, Narraboth,
look at me.
Ah, you know too well
that you will
do as I ask.
You know it well.
I know that you will do it.

Narraboth:
Laßt den Propheten herauskommen.
Die Prinzessin Salome
wünscht ihn zu sehn.

Narraboth: *(signaling the soldiers)*
Let the Prophet out.
Princess Salome
wishes to see him.

Salome:
Ah!

Salome:
Ah!

The Prophet emerges from the cistern. Salome looks at him and recoils slowly.

Solemnly

Molto espressivo

Jochanaan:
Wo ist er, dessen Sündenbecher
jetzt voll ist?
Wo ist er, der eines Tages
im Angesicht alles Volkes
in einem Silbermantel sterben wird?
Heißt ihn herkommen,
auf daß er die Stimme Dessen höre,
der in den Wüsten
und in den Häusern
der Könige gekündet hat.

Jokanaan:
Where is he whose cup of sins overflows?
Where is he, who,
wearing a silver robe,
will one day die before all people?
Let him come forward
that he may hear the voice
of one who cried aloud
in the desert
and in the houses of kings.

Salome:
Von wem spricht er?

Salome: *(to Narraboth)*
Of whom does he speak?

Narraboth:
Niemand kann es sagen, Prinzessin.

Narraboth:
Nobody can tell, Princess.

Jochanaan:
Wo ist sie,
die sich hingab
der Lust ihrer Augen,
die gestanden hat vor buntgemalten
Männerbildern und Gesandte
ins Land der Chaldäer schickte?

Jokanaan:
Where is she,
who surrendered
to the lust in her eyes,
when she stood before images
of painted men and sent
ambassadors into the land of Chaldea?

Salome:
Es spricht von meiner Mutter.

Narraboth:
Nein, nein, Prinzessin.

Salome:
Ja, er spricht von meiner Mutter.

Jochanaan:
Wo ist sie, die den Hauptleuten
Assyriens sich gab?
Wo ist sie, die sich den jungen Männern
der Ägypter gegeben hat, die in feinen
Leinen und Hyacinthgesteinen prangen,
deren Schilde von Gold sind
und die Leiber wie Riesen?

Geht, heißt sie aufstehen
vom Bett ihrer Greuel,
vom Bett ihrer Blutschande;
auf daß sie die Worte
Dessen vernehme,
der dem Herrn die Wege bereitet,
und ihre Missetaten bereue.
Und wenn sie gleich nicht bereut,
heißt sie herkommen,
denn die Geißel
des Herrn ist in seiner Hand.

Salome:
He is talking about my mother.

Narraboth:
No, no, Princess.

Salome:
Yes, he is talking about my mother.

Jokanaan:
Where is she who gave herself to the
leaders of Assyria?
Where is she who gave herself to the
young men of Egypt, with their fine
linens and precious jewels,
their golden shields
and bodies like giants?

Let her rise from her bed
of incest,
the bed of her abominations,
so that she may hear
the words of the One
who prepares the way of the Lord,
and that she may repent of her sins.
And even if she repents,
let her come,
for the scourge of the Lord
is in his hand.

Animato

Salome:
Er ist schrecklich.
Er ist wirklich schrecklich.

Narraboth:
Bleibt nicht hier, Prinzessin,
ich bitte Euch!

Salome:
He is terrifying.
He is really terrifying.

Narraboth:
Don't stay here, Princess,
I beg you!

Salome:
Seine Augen sind von allem
das Schrecklichste.
Sie sind wie die schwarzen Höhlen,
wo die Drachen hausen!
Sie sind wie schwarze Seen,
aus denen irres Mondlicht flackert.

Glaubt ihr, daß er noch einmal
sprechen wird?

Narraboth:
Bleibt nicht hier, Prinzessin, ich bitte
Euch, bleibt nicht hier.

Salome:
Wie abgezehrt er ist!
Er ist wie ein Bildnis aus Elfenbein.
Gewiß ist er keusch wie der Mond.
Sein Fleisch muß sehr kühl sein,
kühl wie Elfenbein.
Ich möchte ihn näher beseh'n.

Narraboth:
Nein, nein, Prinzessin.

Salome:
Ich muß ihn näher beseh'n.

Narraboth:
Prinzessin! Prinzessin!

Jochanaan:
Wer ist dies Weib, das mich ansieht?
Ich will ihre Augen
nicht auf mir haben.
Warum sieht sie mich so an
mit ihren Goldaugen
unter den gleißenden Lidern?
Ich weiß nicht, wer sie ist.
Ich will nicht wissen, wer sie ist.
Heißt sie gehn!
Zu ihr will ich nicht sprechen.

Salome:
His eyes are the most terrifying thing
about him.
They are like the black caverns, where
the dragons make their lair!
They are like black lakes from which
fantastic moons rise.

(to Narraboth)
Do you think he will speak again?

Narraboth:
Don't stay here, Princess, I beg you not
to stay here.

Salome:
How gaunt he is!
He's like an ivory statue.
I'm sure he's as chaste as the moon.
His flesh must be as cool
as ivory.
I must look closer at him.

Narraboth:
No, no, Princess.

Salome:
I must look closer at him.

Narraboth:
Princess, Princess!

Jokanaan:
Who is this women looking at me?
I will not have her eyes
gaze upon me.
Why does she look at me with her
golden eyes
under gilded eyelids?
I do not know who she is.
I do not wish to know who she is.
Bid her go!
I do not wish to speak to her.

Salome:
Ich bin Salome, die Tochter der
Herodias, Prinzessin von Judäa.

Jochanaan:
Zurück, Tochter Babylons!
Komm dem Erwählten des Herrn nicht
nahe!
Deine Mutter hat die Erde erfüllt mit
dem Wein ihrer Lüste, und das Unmass
ihrer Sündenschreit zu Gott.

Salome:
Sprich mehr, Jochanaan,deine Stimme
ist wie Musikin meinen Ohren.

Narraboth:
Prinzessin! Prinzessin! Prinzessin!

Salome:
Sprich mehr, sprich mehr, Jochanaan,
und sag' mir, was ich tun soll?

Jochanaan:
Tochter Sodoms, komm mir nicht nahe!
Vielmehr bedecke dein Gesichtmit
einem Schleier,
streue Asche auf deinem Kopf,
mach' dich auf in die Wüsteund suche
des Menschen Sohn!

Salome:
Wer ist das, des Menschen Sohn?
Ist er so schön wie du, Jochanaan?

Jochanaan:
Weiche von mir!
Ich höre die Flügel
des Todesengels im Palaste rauschen.

Salome:
Jochanaan!

Narraboth:
Prinzessin, ich flehe, geh' hinein!

Salome:
I am Salome, daughter of Herodias,
Princes of Judaea.

Jokanaan:
Stand back, daughter of Babylon!
Do not come near the Lord's chosen
one!
Your mother has filled the earth with the
wine of her iniquities, and God has
heard the cry of her sins.

Salome:
Speak again, Jokanaan, your voice is
like music to my ears.

Narraboth:
Princess! Princess! Princess!

Salome:
Speak again, speak again Jokanaan,
and tell me what I must do?

Jokanaan:
Daughter of Sodom, do not come near me!
Cover your face with a veil
and scatter ashes
over your head:
go out into the wilderness,
and seek the Son of Man!

Salome:
Who is He, the Son of Man?
Is He as beautiful as you, Jokanaan?

Jokanaan:
Get away from me!
I can hear the beating of the wings of
the angel of death in the palace.

Salome:
Jokanaan!

Narraboth:
Princess, I beg you to go inside!

Salome:
Jochanaan! Ich bin verliebt in deinen
Leib, Jochanaan!
Dein Leib ist weiß wie die Lilien
auf einem Felde,
von der Sichel nie berührt.

Dein Leib ist weiß
wie der Schnee
auf den Bergen Judäas.

Die Rosen im Garten
von Arabiens Königin
sind nicht so weiß wie dein Leib,
nicht die Rosen
im Garten der Königin,
nicht die Füße der Dämmerung
auf den Blättern,
nicht die Brüste des Mondes
auf dem Meere.
Nichts in der Welt ist so weiß wie
dein Leib.
Laß mich ihn berühren deinen Leib.

Jochanaan:
Zurück, Tochter Babylons!
Durch das Weib kam
das Übel in die Welt.
Sprich nicht zu mir.
Ich will dich nicht anhör'n!
Ich höre nur
auf die Stimme des Herrn,
meines Gottes.

Salome:
Dein Leib ist grauenvoll.
Er ist wie der Leib
eines Aussätzigen.
Er ist wie eine getünchte Wand,
wo Nattern gekrochen sind;
wie eine getünchte Wand,
wo Skorpione ihr Nest gebaut.
Er ist wie ein übertünchtes Grab
voll widerlicher Dinge.
Er ist gräßlich,
dein Leib ist gr ßlich.

Salome:
Jokanaan! I am in love with your body,
Jokanaan!
Your body is as white as the lilies
of a field
that has not been mowed.

You body is as white
as the snows
on the mountains of Judaea.

The roses in the garden
of the Queen of Arabia
are not as white as your body,
nor the roses
in the garden of Arabia's Queen,
when the leaves fall
at dawn,
nor the moon
when she lies on the sea.
There is nothing in this world
as white as your body.
Let me touch your body.

Jokanaan:
Stand back, daughter of Babylon!
Evil came into the world
by woman.
Do not speak to me.
I will not listen to you!
I listen
only to the voice
of the Lord, my God.

Salome:
Your body is hideous.
It is like the body
of a leper.
It is like a plastered wall
where snakes have crawled,
where scorpions
have made their nest.
It is like a whitened sepulcher,
full of loathsome things.
It is horrible;
your body is horrible.

In dein Haar bin ich verliebt,
Jochanaan.
Dein Haar ist wie Weintrauben,
wie Büschel schwarzer Trauben,
an den Weinstöcken Edoms.
Dein Haar ist wie die Cedern,
die großen Cedern von Libanon,
die den Löwen und Räubern
Schatten spenden.

Die langen schwarzen Nächte,
wenn der Mond sich verbirgt,
wenn die Sterne bangen,
sind nicht so schwarz wie dein Haar.

Des Waldes Schweigen.
Nichts in der Welt
ist so schwarz wie dein Haar.
Laß mich es berühren, dein Haar!

Jochanaan:
Zurück, Tochter Sodoms!
Berühre mich nicht!
Entweihe nicht
den Tempel des Herrn,
meines Gottes!

Salome:
Dein Haar ist gräßlich!
Es starrt von Staub und Unrat.
Es ist wie eine Dornenkroneauf
deinen Kopf gesetzt.
Es ist wie ein
Schlangenknotengewickelt
um deinen Hals.
Ich liebe dein Haar nicht.

Deinen Mund begehre ich, Jochanaan.
Dein Mund ist wie ein Scharlachbandan
einem Turm von Elfenbein.
Er ist wie ein Granatapfelvon
einem Silbermesser zerteilt.
Die Granatapfelblüten in den Gärtenvon
Tyrus,
glüh'nder als Rosen, sind nicht so rot.

It's your hair that I love,
Jokanaan.
Your hair is like bunches of grapes,
like bunches of black grapes that hang
from the vine-trees of Edom.
Your hair is like
the mighty cedars of Lebanon,
that give shade
to lions and robbers.

The long black nights, when the moon
hides her face,
and the stars are afraid,
are not as black as your hair.

The silence of forests.
Nothing in the world
is as black as your hair.
Let me touch your hair!

Jokanaan:
Get back, daughter of Sodom!
Do not touch me!
Do not profane
the temple of the Lord,
Almighty God!

Salome:
Your hair is horrible!
It is thick with dirt and dust.
It is just like a crown of thorns
on your head.
It is like a knot
of black serpents
writhing around your neck.
I do not like your hair.

It is your mouth that I desire, Jokanaan.
Your mouth is like a band of scarlet
on a tower of ivory.
It is like a pomegranate
cut with an ivory knife.
The pomegranates that bloom
in the garden of Tyre,
redder than roses, are not so red.

Die roten Fanfaren der Trompeten,
die das Nah'n von Kön'gen kündenund
vor denen der Feind erzittert,
sind nicht so rot wie dein roter Mund.

Dein Mund ist röter als die Füßeder
Männer die den Wein stampfen in der
Kelter.
Er ist röter als die Füße der Tauben,
die in den Tempeln wohnen.
Dein Mund ist wie ein Korallenzweigin
der Dämm'rung des Meers,
wie der Purpur in den Gruben von Moab,
der Purpur der Könige.
Nichts in der Welt
ist so rot wie dein Mund.
Laß mich ihn küssen, deinen Mund.

Jochanaan:
Niemals, Tochter Babylons,
Tochter Sodoms! Niemals!

Salome:
Ich will deinen Mund küssen,
Jochanaan. Ich will deinen Mund
küssen.

The red fanfares of the trumpets that
herald the approach of kings in wartime
and place fear in the enemy,
are not as red as your mouth.

Your mouth is redder than the feet of
those who tread the wine, stamping in
the wine-presses.
It is redder than the feet of the doves
that haunt the holy temples.
Your mouth is like a branch of coral
found in the twilight sea;
it is like vermilion that kings take from
the mines of Moab.
There is nothing in the world
as red as your mouth.
Let me kiss your mouth, your mouth.

Jokanaan:
Never, daughter of Babylon!
Daughter of Sodom! Never!

Salome:
I will kiss your mouth, Jokanaan.
I want to kiss your mouth.

Narraboth:
Prinzessin, Prinzessin,
die wie ein Garten von Myrrhen ist,
die die Taube aller Tauben ist,
sieh diesen Mann nicht an.
Sprich nicht solche Worte zu ihm.
Ich kann es nicht ertragen.

Salome:
Ich will deinen Mund küssen, Jochanaan.
 Ich will deinen Mund küssen.

Narraboth:
Princess, Princess,
you who are like a garden of myrrh,
and who are the dove of all doves,
do not look at this man.
Do not speak such words to him.
I cannot bear to hear them.

Salome:
I will kiss your mouth, Jokanaan.
I will kiss your mouth.

Narraboth kills himself and falls between Salome and Jokanaan.

Laß mich deinen Mund küssen,
Jochanaan.

Jochanaan:
Wird dir nicht bange,
Tochter der Herodias?

Salome:
Laß mich deinen Mund küssen,
Jochanaan!

Jochanaan:
Tochter der Unzucht,
es lebt nur Einer,
der dich retten kann.
Geh', such' ihn! Such' ihn!
Er ist in einem Nachen auf dem See
von Galiläa
und redet zu seinen Jüngern.
Knie nieder am Ufer des Sees,
ruf ihn an und rufe ihn beim Namen.
Wenn er zu dir kommt,
und er kommt zu allen, die ihn rufen,
dann bücke dich zu seinen Füßen,
daß er dir deine Sünden vergebe.

Salome:
Laß mich deinen Mund küssen,
Jochanaan!

Jokanaan:
Sei verflucht, Tochter der
blutschänderischen Mutter.
Sei verflucht.

Salome:
Laß mich deinen Mund küssen,
Jochanaan!

Jochanaan:
Ich will dich nicht ansehn.
Du bist verflucht, Salome.
Du bist verflucht. Du bist verflucht!

Let me kiss your mouth,
Jokanaan.

Jokanaan:
Aren't you afraid,
daughter of Herodias?

Salome:
Let me kiss your mouth,
Jokanaan?

Jokanaan:
Daughter of adultery, there is but one
who can save you.
Go, seek Him.
Seek Him!
He is in a boat
on the Sea of Galilee
talking with His disciples.
Kneel down on the shore of the sea,
and call Him by name.
When He comes to you,
and He comes to all who call Him,
bow down before Him,
and ask for absolution of your sins.

Salome: *(in the greatest of despair)*
Let me kiss your mouth,
Jokanaan.

Jokanaan:
You are accursed, daughter of an
incestuous mother.
You are accursed.

Salome:
Let me kiss your mouth,
Jokanaan!

Jokanaan:
I don't want to look at you.
You are accursed, Salome.
You are accursed! You are accursed!

Jokanaan descends into the cistern.
Herod and Herodias have left the banquet and arrive on the terrace.

Herodes:
Wo ist Salome?
Wo ist die Prinzessin?
Warum kam sie nicht wieder
zum Bankett,
wie ich ihr befohlen hatte?
Ah! Da ist sie!

Herod:
Where is Salome?
Where is the Princess?
Why didn't she return
to the banquet
as I ordered her?
Ah! There she is!

Herodias:
Du sollst sie nicht ansehn.
Fortwährend siehst du sie an!

Herodias: *(to Herod)*
You must not look at her.
You're always looking at her!

Herodes:
Wie der Mond
heute Nacht aussieht!
Ist es nicht ein seltsames Bild?
Es sieht aus,
wie ein wahnwitziges Weib,
das überall nach Buhlen sucht.
Wie ein betrunkenes Weib
das durch Wolken taumelt.

Herod:
The moon
looks so strange tonight!
Doesn't she have a strange look?
She is like a mad woman,
looking everywhere
for lovers.
She reels through the clouds
like a drunken woman.

Herodias:
Nein, der Mond ist wie der Mond,
das ist alles.
Wir wollen hineingehn.

Herodias:
No, the moon is like the moon,
that's all.
Let's go inside.

Herodes:
Ich will hier bleiben.
Manassah, leg Teppiche hierher!
Zündet Facklen an!
Ich will noch Wein mit meinen
Gästen trinken!

Herod:
I will stay out here.
Manasseh, lay carpets over there!
Light up torches!
I will drink more wine
with my guests!

Ah! Ich bin ausgeglitten.
Ich bin in Blut getreten,
das ist ein böses Zeichen.
Warum ist hier Blut?
Und dieser Tote?
Wer ist dieser Tote hier?
Wer ist dieser Tote?
Ich will ihn nicht sehn.

Ah! I've slipped.
I've slipped in some blood,
that's a bad omen.
Why is there blood here?
And this body?
What is this body doing here?
Who is this dead man?
I will not look at him.

Erster Soldat:
Es ist unser Hauptmann, Herr.

First Soldier:
It is our captain, Sir.

Herodes:
Ich erließ keinen Befehl,
daß er getötet werde.

Herod:
I didn't order him to be killed.

Erster Soldat:
Er hat sich selbst getötet, Herr.

First Soldier:
He killed himself, Sir.

Herodes:
Das scheint mir seltsam.
Der junge Syrier, er war sehr schön.
Ich erinnre mich,
ich sah seine schmachtenden Augen,
wenn er Salome ansah.
Fort mit ihm!

Herod:
That's odd.
This young Syrian was very handsome.
I remember now,
I saw him look longingly
at Salome.
Take him away!

Narraboth's corpse is removed.

Es ist kalt hier. Es weht ein Wind.
Weht nicht ein Wind?

It's cold here. There's a wind blowing.
Isn't there a wind?

Herodias:
Nein, es weht kein Wind.

Herodias:
No, there's no wind.

Herodes:
Ich sage Euch: es weht ein Wind,
und in der Luft hör ich etwas,
wie das Rauschen
von mächt'gen Flügeln.
Hört ihr es nicht?

Herod:
I'm telling you there is a wind,
and in the air I can hear something
like the beating
of huge wings.
Can't you hear it?

Herodias:
Ich höre nichts.

Herodias:
I hear nothing.

Herodes:
Jetzt höre ich es nicht mehr.
Aber ich habe es gehört.
Es war das Wehn des Windes.
Es ist vorüber.
Horch! Hört ihr es nicht?
Das Rauschen
von mächt'gen Flügeln.

Herod:
I can't hear it now,
but I did hear something.
It was the wind blowing.
But it has stopped now.
Listen! Can you hear it?
It's just like
beating wings.

Herodias:
Du bist krank.
Wir wollen hineingehn.

Herodias:
You're ill.
Let's go inside.

Herodes:
Ich bin nicht krank.
Aber deine Tochter
ist krank zu Tode.
Niemals hab' ich sie so blaß gesehn.

Herod:
I'm not ill.
It 's your daughter
who's sick.
I've never I seen her looking so pale.

Herodias:
Ich habe dir gesagt,
du sollst sie nicht ansehn.

Herodias:
I've told you,
not to look at her.

Herodes:
Schenkt mir Wein ein!
Salome, komm, trink Wein mit mir,
einen köstlichen Wein.

Herod:
Give me some wine!
Salome, come and drink some of this
exquisite wine with me.

Molto animato
HEROD

Sa - lo - me, komm, trink Wein mit mir,

Cäsar selbst hat ihn mir geschickt.
Tauche deine kleinen Lippen hinein,
Deine kleinen roten Lippen,
dann will ich den Becher leeren.

Caesar himself sent it to me.
Dip your little red lips into it,
those little red lips,
so that I may drain the cup.

Salome:
Ich bin nicht durstig, Tetrarch.

Salome:
I'm not thirsty, Tetrarch.

Herodes:
Hörst du, wie sie mir antwortet,
diese deine Tochter?

Herod: *(to Herodias)*
Do you hear how your daughter
answers me?

Herodias:
Sie hat recht.
Warum starrst du sie immer an?

Herodias:
She's right.
Why are you always staring at her?

Herodes:
Bringt reife Früchte!
Salome, komm,
iß mit mir von diese Früchten.
Den Abdruck deiner kleinen
weißen Zähne
in einer Frucht seh' ich so gern.

Herod:
Bring me ripe fruits!
Salome, come,
and eat fruit with me.
I love to see
your little bite marks
in a sweet fruit.

Beiß nur ein wenig ab,
nur ein wenig von dieser Frucht,
dann will ich essen, was übrig ist.

Salome:
Ich bin nicht hungrig, Tetrarch.

Herodes:
Du siehst, wie du diese
deine Tochter erzogen hast!

Herodias:
Meine Tochter und ich stammen
aus königlichem Blut.
Dein Vater war Kameeltreiber,
dein Vater war ein Dieb.
und ein Räuber oben drein.

Herodes:
Salome, komm, setz dich zu mir.
Du sollst auf dem Thron
deiner Mutter sitzen.

Salome:
Ich bin nicht müde, Tetrarch.

Herodias:
Du siehst, wie sie dich achtet.

Herodes:
Bringt mir was wünsche ich denn?
Ich habe es vergessen.
Ah! Ah! Ich erinnre mich.

Die Stimme von Jochanaan:
Sieh', die Zeit ist gekommen,
der Tag von dem ich sprach, ist da.

Herodias:
Heiss' ihn schweigen!
Dieser Mensch beschimpft mich!

Herodes:
Er hat nichts gegen dich gesagt.
Überdies ist er ein sehr großer Prophet.

Just take a little bite,
a little bite of this sweet fruit,
and I will eat what is left.

Salome:
I'm not hungry, Tetrarch.

Herod: *(to Herodias)*
You see, how you reared
this daughter of yours!

Herodias:
My daughter and I are
of royal blood.
Your father was a camel driver,
and your father was
a thief and robber.

Herod:
Salome, come and sit next to me.
I will give you your mother's throne
to sit upon.

Salome:
I'm not tired, Tetrarch.

Herodias:
You see what she thinks of you.

Herod:
Bring me what it is I desire?
I've forgotten what I wanted.
Ah! Ah! I remember now.

The Voice of Jokanaan:
See, the time has come,
the day of which I spoke is here.

Herodias:
Shut him up!
This man always insults me!

Herod:
He has said nothing against you.
Besides, he is a very great Prophet.

Herodias:
Ich glaube nicht an Propheten.
Aber du, du hast Angst vor ihm.

Herodes:
Ich habe vor niemanden Angst.

Herodias:
Ich sage dir, du hast Angst vor ihm.
Warum lieferst du ihn nicht,
den Juden aus,
die seit Monaten nach ihm schreien?

Erster Jude:
Wahrhaftig, Herr, es wäre besser,
ihn in unsre Hände zu geben!

Herodes:
Genug davon!
Ich werde ihn nicht
in Eure Hände geben.
Er ist ein heil'ger Mann.
Er ist ein Mann,
der Gott geschaut hat.

Erster Jude:
Das kann nicht sein.
Seit dem Propheten Elias
hat niemand Gott gesehn.
Er war der letzte,
der Gott von Angesicht geschaut.
In unsern Tagen zeigt sich Gott nicht.
Gott verbirgt sich.
Darum ist großes Übel
über das Land gekommen,
großes Übel.

Zweiter Jude:
In Wahrheit weiß niemand,
ob Elias in der Tat Gott gesehen hat.
Möglicherweise war es nur
der Schatten Gottes, was er sah.

Dritter Jude:
Gott ist zu keiner Zeit verborgen.
Er zeigt sich zu allen Zeiten
und an allen Orten.

Herodias:
I don't believe in Prophets.
But I know you're afraid of him!

Herod:
I'm afraid of no man.

Herodias:
I tell you, you're afraid of him.
Then why don't you
hand him over to the Jews, who have
been screaming for him for months?

First Jew:
Truly, my lord, it would be better to
hand him over to us!

Herod:
Enough of this!
I've already told you
I won't hand him over to you.
He is a holy man.
He is a man
who has seen God.

First Jew:
That cannot be.
No man since the Prophet Elijah
has seen God.
He is the last man
who saw God.
In these times
God hides Himself.
That is why
great evils
have come upon the land.

Second Jew:
And truly, no one really knows if the
Prophet Elijah saw God.
Perhaps it was only the shadow of God
that he saw.

Third Jew:
God is never hidden.
He shows Himself at all times
and in everything.

Gott ist im schlimmen
ebenso wie im guten.

God is in what is good
and what is evil.

Vierter Jude:
Du solltest das nicht sagen,
es ist eine sehr gefährliche Lehre
aus Alexandria.
Und die Griechen sind Heiden.

Fourth Jew: *(to the Third Jew)*
Don't say such things.
It is a very dangerous dogma that comes
from Alexandria.
And from the Greeks are Gentiles.

Funfter Jude:
Niemand kann sagen, wie Gott wirkt.
Seine Wege sind sehr dunkel.
Wir können nur unser Haupt
unter seinen Willen beugen,
denn Gott ist sehr stark.

Fifth Jew:
No one can tell us how God works.
His ways are very mysterious.
We must submit
to all and everything to Him,
for God is very strong.

Erster Jude:
Du sagst die Wahrheit.
Fürwahr, Gott ist furchtbar.
Aber was diesen Menschen angeht,
der hat Gott nie gesehn.
Seit dem Propheten Elias
hat niemand Gott gesehn.

First Jew:
That's true.
God is awe-inspiring.
But this man
has never seen God.
No man has seen God
since the Prophet Elijah.

Herodias:
Heiss' sie schweigen,
sie langweilen mich.

Herodias: *(to Herod)*
Make them be quiet.
They weary me.

Herodes:
Doch' hab ich davon sprechen hören,
Jochanaan sei
in Wahrheit Euer Prophet Elias.

Herod:
I've heard it said
that Jokanaan himself
is your Prophet Elijah.

Erster Jude:
Daß kann nicht sein.
Seit den Tagen des Propheten Elias
sind mehr als
dreihundert Jahre vergangen.

First Jew:
That cannot be,
the prophet Elijah
lived more than
three hundred years ago.

Erster Nazarener:
Mir ist sicher, daß er
der Prophet Elias ist.

First Nazarene:
I'm sure that he is
the Prophet Elijah.

Erster Jude:
Das kann nicht sein...

First Jew:
He cannot be...

Die Anderen Jude:
Keineswegs,
er ist nicht der Prophet Elias.

Herodias:
Heiss' sie schweigen!

Die Stimme von Jochanaan:
Siehe, der Tag ist nahe,
der Tag des Herrn,
und ich höre auf den Bergen
die Schritte Dessen,
der sein wird der Erlöser der Welt.

Herodes:
Was soll das heißen,
der Erlöser der Welt?

Erster Nazarener:
Der Messias ist gekommen.

Erster Jude:
Der Messias ist nicht gekommen.

Erster Nazarener:
Er ist gekommen,
und allenthalben tut er Wunder.
Bei einer Hochzeit in Galiläa
bat er Wasser in Wein verwandelt.
Er heilte zwei Aussätzige
von Kapernaum.

Zweiter Nazarener:
Durch bloßes Berühren!

Erster Nazarener:
Er hat auch Blinde geheilt.
Man hat ihn auf einem Berge
im Gespräch mit Engeln gesehn!

Herodias:
Oho! Ich glaube nicht an Wunder,
ich habe ihrer zu viele gesehn!

Erster Nazarener:
Die Tochter des Jarus
hat er von den Toten erweckt.

The Other Jews:
Not at all,
he is not the Prophet Elijah.

Herodias:
Make them be quiet!

The Voice of Jokanaan:
So the day is come,
the day of the Lord,
and I can hear on the mountains
the feet of Him,
who will be the Savior of the world.

Herod:
What does that mean,
Savior of the world?

First Nazarene:
The Messiah is now come.

First Jew:
The Messiah has not yet come.

First Nazarene:
He has come,
and works miracles everywhere.
He changed water into wine at a
wedding in Galilee.
He healed two lepers
at Capernaeum.

Second Nazarene:
Just by touching them!

First Nazarene:
He also healed blind people.
And he was seen on a mountain
speaking with angels!

Herodias:
Ho! Ho! I don't believe in miracles,
I've seen too many!

First Nazarene:
He raised the daughter of Jairus from
the dead.

Herodes:
Wie, er erweckt die Toten?

Herod:
He raises the dead?

Erster, Zweiter Nazarener:
Jawohl. Er erweckt die Toten.

First, Second Nazarenes:
Yes, Sire, He raises the dead.

Herodes:
Ich verbiete ihm, das zu tun.
Es wäre schrecklich,
wenn die Toten wiederkämen!
Wo ist der Mann zur Zeit?

Herod:
I forbid him to do that.
It would be dreadful
if the dead came to life again!
Where is this man now?

Erster Nazarener:
Herr, er ist überall,
aber es ist schwer, ihn zu finden.

First Nazarene:
Sir, he is everywhere,
but it is hard to find him.

Herodes:
Der Mann muß gefunden werden.

Herod:
He must be found.

Zweiter Nazarener:
Er heißt, in Samaria weile er jetzt.

Second Nazarene:
They say he is in Samaria.

Erster Nazarener:
Vor ein paar Tagen verließ
er Samaria,
ich glaube, im Augenblick ist er
in der Nähe von Jerusalem.

First Nazarene:
But He left Samaria
a few days ago,
and I think He is now
in the neighborhood of Jerusalem.

Herodes:
So hört:
ich verbiete ihm
die Toten zu erwecken!
Es müßte schrecklich sein,
wenn die Toten wiederkämen!

Herod:
Hear me:
I forbid Him
to wake the dead!
It would be terrible
if the dead were brought to life gain!

Die Stimme von Jochanaan:
O, über dieses geile Weib,
die Tochter Babylons,
so spricht der Herr, unser Gott!

The Voice of Jokanaan:
Ah! The harlot, that daughter of
Babylon,
thus speaks the Lord, our God.

Herodias:
Befiehl ihm, er soll schweigen.

Herodias:
Tell him to be quiet.

Die Stimme von Jochanaan:
Eine Menge Menschen wird
sich gegen sie sammeln,

The Voice of Jokanaan:
A multitude will rise
against her,

und sie werden Steine nehmen
und sie steinigen!

and take up stones
and stone her to death!

Herodias:
Wahrhaftig, er ist schändlich!

Herodias:
You hear that, this is outrageous!

Die Stimme von Jochanaan:
Die Kriegshauptleute
werden sie mit ihren Schwertern
durchbohren,
sie werden sie mit ihren Schilden
zermalmen!

The Voice of Jokanaan:
Their captains
will pierce her
with their sharp swords
and crush her
beneath their heavy shields!

Herodias:
Er soll schweigen! Er soll schweigen!

Herodias:
This is outrageous! This is outrageous!

Die Stimme von Jochanaan:
Es ist so, daß ich alle Verruchtheit
austilgen werde
daß ich alle Weiber lehren werde,
nicht auf den Wegen ihrer Greuel
zu wandeln!

The Voice of Jokanaan:
And thus I will wipe out
all wickedness from the earth,
and all women
shall learn not to imitate
her abominations!

Herodias:
Du hörst, was er gegen mich sagt,
du duldest es, daß er die schmähe,
die dein Weib ist?

Herodias:
Do you hear what he says against me?
Do you allow him
to slander your wife?

Herodes:
Er hat deinem Namen nicht genannt.

Herod:
He didn't speak your name.

Die Stimme von Jochanaan:
Es kommt ein Tag,
da wird die Sonne
finster werden wie
ein schwarzes Tuch.
Und der Mond
wird werden wie Blut,
und die Sterne des Himmels
werden zur Erde fallen
wie unreife Feigen
vom Feigenbaum.
Es kommt ein Tag, wo die Kön'ge
der Erde erzittern.

The Voice of Jokanaan:
On that day,
the sun
shall turn black
as a sackcloth,
and the moon
shall become like blood,
and the stars
shall fall to the earth
like ripe figs
from the fig tree.
On that day, the kings of the earth shall
be afraid.

Herodias:
Ha, ha! Dieser Prophet

Herodias:
Ah! Ah! This Prophet

schwatzt wie ein Betrunkener.
Aber ich kann den Klang
seiner Stimme nicht ertragen,
ich hasse seine Stimme.
Befiehl ihm, er soll schweigen.

Herodes:
Tanz für mich, Salome.

Herodias:
Ich will nicht haben, daß sie tanzt.

Salome:
Ich habe keine Lust zu tanzen, Tetrarch.

Herodes:
Salome Tochter der Herodias,
tanz für mich!

Salome:
Ich will nicht tanzen, Tetrarch.

Herodias:
Du siehst, wie sie dir gehorcht.

Die Stimme von Jochanaan:
Er wird auf seinem Throne sitzen,
er wird gekleidet sein
in Scharlach und Purpur.
Und der Engel de Herrn
wird ihn darniederschlagen.
Er wird von den Würmern
gefressen werden.

Herodes:
Salome, Salome, tanz für mich,
ich bitte dich.
Ich bin traurig heute Nacht,
drum tanz für mich.
Salome, tanz für mich!
Wenn du für mich tanzest,
kannst du von mir begehren
was du willst.
Ich werde es dir geben.

talks like a drunken man.
I cannot stand
the sound of his voice;
I hate this voice.
Make him be quiet.

Herod:
Dance for me, Salome.

Herodias:
I will not let her dance.

Salome:
I have no desire to dance, Tetrarch.

Herod:
Salome, daughter of Herodias,
dance for me!

Salome:
I will not dance, Tetrarch.

Herodias:
You see how she obeys you.

The Voice of Jokanaan:
He shall be seated upon his throne,
and he shall be clothed
in scarlet and purple.
And the angel of the Lord
shall smite him.
And the worms
shall feed on him

Herod:
Salome, Salome, dance for me,
I beg you.
I am very sad tonight,
so dance for me.
Salome, dance for me!
If you dance for me
you may ask of me
whatever you want.
I'll give you what you ask for.

Salome:
Willst du mir wirklich alles geben,
was ich von dir begehre, Tetrarch?

Herodias:
Tanze nicht, meine Tochter.

Herodes:
Alles, alles,
was du von mir begehren wirst,
und wär's die
Hälfte meines Königreichs.

Salome:
Du schwörst, Tetrarch?

Herodes:
Ich schwör' es, Salome.

Salome:
Wobei willst du das beschwören,
Tetrarch?

Herodes:
Bei meinem Leben,
bei meiner Krone,
bei meinen Göttern.

Herodias:
Tanze nicht, meine Tochter!

Herodes:
O Salome, Salome, tanz für mich!

Salome:
Du hast einen Eid Geschworen,
Tetrarch.

Herodes:
Ich habe einen Eid geschworen.

Herodias:
Meine Tochter, tanze nicht.

Herodes:
Und wär's die Hälfte
meines Königreichs.

Salome:
Tetrarch, will you really give me
whatever I   ask?

Herodias:
Do not dance, my daughter.

Herod:
Everything, everything,
that you ask for,
even half
of my kingdom.

Salome:
You swear it, Tetrarch?

Herod:
I swear it, Salome.

Salome:
By what will you swear by,
Tetrarch?

Herod:
By my life,
by my crown,
by my gods.

Herodias:
Do not dance, my daughter!

Herod:
Salome, Salome, dance for me!

Salome:
You have sworn an oath,
Tetrarch.

Herod:
I have sworn an oath.

Herodias:
My daughter, do not dance.

Herod:
Even half
of my kingdom.

Du wirst schön sein als Königin,
unermeßlich schön.

Ah! Es ist kalt hier.
Es weht ein eis'ger Wind,
und ich höre
warum höre ich in der Luft
dieses Rauschen von Flügeln?

Ah! Es ist doch so,
als ob ein ungeheurer,
schwarzer Vogel über der
Terrasse schwebte?
Warum kann ich ihn nicht sehn,
diesen Vogel?
Dieses Rauschen ist schrecklich.
Es ist ein schneidender Wind.
Aber nein, er ist nicht kalt,
er ist heiß.
Gießt mir Wasser über die Hände,
gebt mir Schnee zu essen,
macht mir den Mantel los.
Schnell, schnell,
macht mir den Mantel los!
Doch nein! Laßt ihn!
Dieser Kranz drückt mich.
Diese Rosen sind wie Feuer.

You will make a lovely queen,
and so beautiful.

Ah! It's cold here.
There's an icy wind,
and I hear something:
why do I hear
the beating of wings in the air?

Ah! It is as though
there's a huge black bird;
is it hovering,
over the terrace?
Why can't I
see this bird?
The beating wings are terrible;
there's a chill wind.
But no, it's not cold,
it's hot.
Pour water over my hands.
Give me snow to eat,
loosen my cloak.
Quick, quick,
loosen my cloak!
No, leave them!
It's my crown that hurts me.
Ah! Those roses are like fire.

Herod convulsively tears the wreath from his head and throws it to the ground.

Ah! Jetzt kann ich atmen.
Jetzt bin ich glücklich.
Willst du für mich tanzen, Salome?

Ah! I can breathe now.
I'm happy now.
Will you dance for me, Salome?

Herodias:
Ich will nicht haben, daß sie tanze!

Herodias:
I will not have it that she dances!

Salome:
Ich will für dich tanzen.

Salome:
I'll dance for you, Tetrarch.

Slaves bring perfumes and the seven veils, and Salome removes her sandals.

Die Stimme von Jochanaan:
Wer ist der, der von Edom kommt?
Wer ist der, der von Bosra kommt,
dessen Kleid mit Purpur gefärbt ist,
der in der Schönheit seiner

The Voice of Jokanaan:
Who is this who comes from Edom?
Who is this who comes from Bozra?
And whose raiment is dyed with purple,
who is the beauty of his garments

Gewänder leuchtet,
der mächtig
in seiner Größe wandelt?
Warum ist dein Kleid mit
Scharlach gefleckt?

shineth
that might
walk in His greatness?
Why is your raiment
stained with scarlet?

Herodias:
Wir wollen hineingehn.
Die Stimme dieses Menschen
macht mich wahnsinnig.
Ich will nicht haben,
daß meine Tochter tanzt,
während er immer
dazwischen schreit.
Ich will nicht haben, daß sie tanzt,
während du sie
auf solche Art ansiehst.
Mit einem Wort:
Ich will nicht haben, daß sie tanzt.

Herodias:
Let us go inside.
The voice of that man
maddens me.
I will not have
my daughter dance
while he
keeps crying out.
I will not have her dance
while you look at her
in that way.
In short, I will not have my daughter
dance.

Herodes:
Steh nicht auf, mein Weib,
meine Königin.
Es wird dir nichts helfen,
ich gehe nicht hinein,
bevor sie getanzt hat.
Tanze, Salome, tanz für mich!

Herod:
Do not get up, my wife,
my queen,
it will do you no good.
I will not go inside
until she has danced.
Dance, Salome, dance for me!

Herodias:
Tanze nicht, meine Tochter!

Herodias:
Don't dance, my dear daughter!

Salome:
Ich bin bereit, Tetrarch.

Salome:
I am ready, Tetrarch.

The musicians begin. Salome stands motionless. She rises to her full height and makes a sign to the musicians. They subdue the wild rhythm instantly and play a soft and swaying tune. Salome dances the Dance of the Seven Veils.

Salome seems to faint for a moment. Then she pulls herself together with renewed strength. She remains for an instant in a visionary attitude near the cistern where Jokanaan is kept prisoner. Then she throws herself at Herod's feet.

Herodes:
Ah! Herrlich!
Wundervoll, wundervoll!
Siehst du,
sie hat für mich getanzt,
deine Tochter.

Komm her, Salome. Komm her,
du sollst deinen Lohn haben.
Ich will dich königlich belohnen.
Ich will dir alles geben,
was dein Herz begehrt.
Was willst du haben? Sprich!

Salome:
Ich möchte, daß sie mir gleich
in einer Silberschüssel...

Herodes:
In einer Silberschüssel...
Gewiß doch...
in einer Silberschüssel.
Sie ist reizend, nicht?
Was ist's,
das du in einer Silberschüssel
haben möchtest,
o süße, schöne Salome,

Herod:
Ah! Wonderful!
Wonderful, wonderful!
Ah! You see,
your fair daughter
has danced for me.

Come, Salome, come,
so that I can reward you.
I'll pay you royally.
I'll give you
whatever you want.
Tell me what you want? Speak!

Salome:
I want someone to bring me
on a silver platter...

Herod:
On a silver platter....
surely,
on a silver platter.
Isn't she charming?
What is it
that you want on a silver platter,
say what it is.
Oh sweet, fair Salome,

du, die schöner ist
als alle Töchter Judäas?
Was sollen sie dir
in einer Silberschüssel bringen?
Sag es mir!
Was es auch sein mag,
du sollst es erhalten.
Meine Reichtümer gehören dir.
Was ist es,
das du haben möchtest, Salome?

you, who are fairer
than all the daughters of Judaea?
What do you want
to be brought on a silver charger?
Tell me now!
Whatever it is,
you shall have it.
All my treasure, they belong to you.
What is it,
that you want, Salome?

Salome:
Den Kopf des Jochanaan.

Salome:
The head of Jokanaan.

Herodes:
Nein, nein!

Herod:
No, no!

Herodias:
Ah! Das sagst du gut, meine Tochter!
Das sagst du gut!

Herodias:
Ah! That's well said, my daughter!
That's well said!

Herodes:
Nein, nein, Salome!
Das ist es nicht, was du begehrst!
Hör nicht auf
die Stimme deiner Mutter.
Sie gab dir immer schlechten Rat.
Achte nicht auf sie.

Herod:
No, no, Salome!
Don't ask that of me!
Don't listen
to the voice of your mother.
She's always giving you bad advice.
Don't listen to her.

Salome:
Ich achte nicht auf die Stimme
meiner Mutter.
Zu meiner eignen Lust
will ich den Kopf des Jochanaan
in einer Silberschüssel haben.
Du hast einen Eid geschworen,
Du hast einen Eid geschworen.
Vergiß das nicht!

Salome:
I don't listen to
the voice of my mother.
It is for my own pleasure
that I ask for Jokanaan's
head on a silver platter.
You have sworn an oath.
You have sworn an oath.
Remember that well!

Herodes:
Ich weiß,
ich habe einen Eid geschworen.
Ich weiß es wohl.
Bei meinen Göttern habe ich
es geschworen.
Aber ich beschwöre dich, Salome,
verlange etwas andres von mir.

Herod:
I know very well,
that I have sworn an oath.
I know it well.
I have sworn an oath,
by my gods.
But I beg you, Salome,
to ask me for something else.

Verlange die Hälfte
meines Königreichs.
Ich will sie dir geben.
Aber verlange nicht von mir,
was deine Lippen verlangten.

Salome:
Ich verlange von dir den Kopf
des Jochanaan.

Herodes:
Nein, nein,
ich will ihn dir nicht geben.

Salome:
Du hast einen Eid geschworen,
Herodes.

Herodias:
Ja, du hast einen Eid geschworen.
Alle haben es gehört.

Herodes:
Still, Weib,
zu dir spreche ich nicht.

Herodias:
Meine Tochter hat recht daran getan,
den Kopf des Jochanaan zu verlangen.
Er hat mich mit Schimpf
und Schande bedeckt.
Man kann sehn,
daß sie ihre Mutter liebt.
Gib nicht nach, meine Tochter,
gib nicht nach!
Er hat einen Eid geschworen.

Herodes:
Still, spricht nicht zu mir!
Salome, ich beschwöre dich:
sei nicht trotzig! Sieh,
ich habe dich immer lieb gehabt.
Kann sein,
ich habe dich zu lieb gehabt.
Darum verlange das nicht von mir.

Ask me
for half of my kingdom,
I will give it to you.
But don't ask of me
what your lips have just uttered.

Salome:
I ask of you for the head of Jokanaan.

Herod:
No, no,
I won't give it to you.

Salome:
You have sworn an oath,
Herod.

Herodias:
Yes, you have sworn an oath.
Everybody heard you.

Herod:
Be quiet, woman,
I'm not talking to you.

Herodias:
My daughter has done well
to ask for the head of Jokanaan.
He has said
monstrous things about me.
One can see
that she loves her mother well.
Don't give in, my daughter,
don't give in!
He has sworn an oath.

Herod:
Quiet. I'm not talking to you!
Salome, I beg of you
to be reasonable!
I have always loved you.
Perhaps,
I have loved you too much.
So please don't ask this thing of me.

Der Kopf eines Mannes,
der vom Rumpf getrennt ist,
ist ein übler Anblick.
Hör', was ich sage!
Ich habe einen Smaragd.
Er ist der schönste Smaragd
der ganzen Welt.
Den willst du haben, nicht wahr?
Verlang' ihn von mir,
ich will ihn dir geben,
den schönsten Smaragd.

Salome:
Ich fordre den Kopf des Jochanaan!

Herodes:
Du hörst nicht zu,
du hörst nicht zu.
Laß mich zu dir reden, Salome!

Salome:
Den Kopf des Jochanaan.

Herodes:
Das sagst du nur, um mich zu quälen,
weil ich dich so angeschaut habe.
Deine Schönheit hat mich verwirrt.
Oh! Oh! Bringt Wein! Mich dürstet!
Salome, Salome,
laß uns wie Freunde
zu einander sein!
Bedenk' dich!
Ah! Was wollt ich sagen?
Was war's?
Ah! Ich weiß es wieder!
Salome,
du kennst meine weißen Pfauen,
meine schönen, weißen Pfauen,
die im Garten zwischen
den Myrten wandeln.
Ich will sie dir alle, alle geben.
In der ganzen Welt lebt kein König,
der solche Pfauen hat.
Ich habe bloß hundert.
Aber alle will ich dir geben.

The head of a man,
that is cut from its body
is too horrible to look at.
Listen to what I tell you!
I have an emerald.
It is the finest
in the whole world.
You would like that, wouldn't you?
Ask me for it,
and I'll give it to you,
the finest emerald.

Salome:
I want the head of Jokanaan.

Herod:
You're not listening,
you're not listening.
Let me speak, Salome!

Salome:
The head of Jokanaan.

Herod:
You're saying that to annoy me,
because I've been
looking at you.
Bring me wine, I'm thirsty!
Salome, Salome,
let's be friends,
come closer to me!
You should think!
Ah! What was I about to say?
What was it?
Ah! I remember!
Salome,
you know my beautiful white peacocks,
my beautiful white peacocks that walk
in the garden
among the myrtles.
I'll give them all to you.
No king in the world
has peacocks like mine.
I have only a hundred of them.
But I will give them all to you.

Salome:
Gib mir den Kopf des Jochanaan!

Herodias:
Gut gesagt, meine Tochter!

Herodes:
Still, Weib!
Du kreischest wie ein Raubvogel.

Herodias:
Und du, du bist lächerlich
mit deinem Pfauen.

Herodes:
Deine Stimme peinigt mich.
Still, sag' ich dir!
Salome, bedenk, was du tun willst.
Es kann sein,
daß der Mann von Gott gesandt ist.
Er ist ein heil'ger Mann.
Der Finger Gottes hat ihn berührt.
Du möchtest nicht,
daß mich ein Unheil trifft, Salome?
Hör' jetzt auf mich!

Salome:
Ich will den Kopf des Jochanaan.

Herodes:
Ah! Du willst nicht auf mich hören.
Sei ruhig, Salome.
Ich, siehst du, bin ruhig. Höre:
ich habe an diesem
Ort Juwelen versteckt,
Juwelen, die selbst deine Mutter nie
gesehen hat.
Ich habe ein Halsband mit
vier Reihen Perlen.
Topase,
gelb wie die Augen der Tiger.
Topase, hellrot
wie die Augen der Waldtaube,
und grüne Topase, wie Katzenaugen.

Ich habe Opale, die immer funkeln,
mit einem Feuer, kalt wie Eis.

Salome:
Give me the head of Jokanaan!

Herodias:
Well said, my daughter!

Herod:
Silence, wife!
You cry out like a beast of prey.

Herodias:
And you, you and your
peacocks are ridiculous.

Herod:
I'm tired of listening to you.
Quiet, I tell you!
Salome, think of what you're doing.
People say
perhaps this man has been sent by God.
He is a holy man.
The finger of God has touched him.
Salome, you wouldn't want
something terrible to happen to me?
Listen to me!

Salome:
Give me the head of Jokanaan.

Herod:
Ah! You're not listening to me.
Be calm, Salome.
I am calm, as you can see, so listen:
I have jewels hidden here
marvelous jewels
that not even
your mother has ever seen.
I have a collar
of pearls set in four rows.
Topazes,
yellow like the eyes of a tiger.
Topazes as pink,
as the eyes of a wood-pigeon, and
green topazes, like Persian cats' eyes.

I have opals that burn
with an ice-like flame.

Ich will sie dir alle geben, alle!
Ich habe Chrysolithe und Berylle,
Chrysoprase und Rubine.
Ich habe Sardonyx
und Hyacinthsteine
und Steine von Chalcedon.
Ich will sie dir alle geben,
alle und noch andre Dinge.

Ich habe einen Kristall
in den zu schaun keinem
Weibe vergönnt ist.
In einem Perlenmutterkästchen
habe ich drei wunderbare Türkise:
wer sie an seiner Stirne trägt,
kann Dinge sehn,
die nicht wirklich sind.

Es sind unbezahlbare Schätze.
Was begehrst du sonst noch, Salome?
Alles, was du verlangst,
will ich dir geben
nur eines nicht:
nur nicht das Leben
dieses einen Mannes.
Ich will dir den Mantel
des Hohenpriesters geben.
Ich will dir den Vorhang
des Allerheiligsten geben.

Die Juden:
Oh! Oh! Oh!

Salome:
Gib' mir den Kopf den Jochanaan!

Herodes:
Man soll ihr geben, was sie verlangt!
Sie ist in Wahrheit ihrer
Mutter Kind!

I will give them all to you, all!
I have chrysolites and beryls,
chrysoprases and rubies.
I have some sardonyx,
and hyacinth stones,
also stones of chalcedony,
and I will give them all to you,
and I'll add others.

I have a crystal
into which women
are forbidden to look.
In a mother-of-pearl box, I'm holding
three little wonderful turquoises:
Whoever wears them on his forehead
can see things
that are not there.

These are priceless treasures.
Salome, what more could you want?
Ah! Whatever you ask for,
I'll gladly give you all,
except one thing:
I won't give you
a man's life.
I'll give you the cloak
of the High Priest.
I'll give you
the veil of the holy sanctuary.

The Jews:
Oh! Oh! Oh!

Salome:
Give me the head of Jokanaan!

Herod: *(in despair)*
Let her be given what she wants!
She is indeed
her mother's child!

Herodias draws the Ring of Death from Herod and gives it to the first soldier,
who immediately brings it to the Executioner.

Wer hat meinen Ring genommen?

Who has taken my ring from me?

The Executioner descends into the cistern.

Ich hatte einen Ring an meiner rechten Hand.	I surely had a ring on my right hand.
Wer hat meinen Wein getrunken?	Who has drunk my wine?
Es war Wein in meinem Becher.	There was wine in my cup.
Er war mit Wein gefüllt.	It was full of wine.
Es hat ihn jemand ausgetrunken.	Somebody has drunk it.
Oh! gewiß wird Unheil über einen kommen.	Oh! I'm sure, some misfortune will surely fall upon us.

Herodias:

Meine Tochter hat recht getan!

Herodias:

My daughter has done well!

Herodes:

Ich bin sicher,
es wird ein Unheil geschehn.

Herod:

I am certain that some misfortune will happen.

Salome leans over the cistern and listens intently.

Salome:

Es ist kein Laut zu vernehmen.
Ich höre nichts.
Warum schreit er nicht, der Mann?
Ah! Wenn einer mich zu töten käme,
ich würde schreien,
ich würde mich wehren,
ich würde es nicht dulden!
Schlag' zu, schlag' zu, Naaman!
Schlag' zu, sag' ich dir!
Nein, ich höre nichts.
Es ist eine schreckliche Stille!
Ah! Es ist etwas zu Boden gefallen.
Ich hörte etwas fallen.
Er hat das Schwert fallen lassen!
Er trautsich nicht, ihn zu töten.
Er ist eine Memme, dieser Sklave.
Schickt Soldaten ihn!

Salome:

There's no sound. I hear nothing.
There's not a sound.
Why doesn't this man cry out?
Ah! If any man tried to kill me,
I would cry out.
I would struggle;
I would not be able to bear it!
Strike, strike, Naaman!
Strike now, I tell you!
No, I hear nothing.
There is a terrible silence!
Ah! I heard something fall to the ground.
I heard something fall.
It was the executioner's sword!
He's afraid to behead him.
He's a coward, this weak executioner.
Send some soldiers down!

(to the Page)

Komm hierher,
du warst der Freund dieses Toten, nicht?
Wohlan, ich sage dir:
es sind noch nicht genug Tote.
Geh zu den Soldaten
und befiehl ihnen,
hinabzusteigen und mir zu holen,
was ich verlange, was der Tetrarch
mir versprochen hat, was mein ist!

Come here,
weren't you the friend of the dead man?
Well, let me tell you
that there aren't enough dead men.
Quick, go to the soldiers,
and order them,
to go down and bring me what I want:
what the Tetrarch promised me;
the thing that is mine!

(to the Soldiers)

Hierher, ihr Soldaten,
geht ihr in die Cisterne hinunter
und holt mir den Kopf des Mannes!
Tetrarch, Tetrarch,
befiehl deinen Soldaten,
daß sie mir den
Kopf des Jochanaan holen!

Come here, soldiers, go down into the
cistern and bring me
the head of this man!
Tetrarch, Tetrarch,
order your soldiers
to bring me
the head of Jokanaan!

A huge black arm of the Executioner emerges from the cistern,
bearing the head of Jokanaan on a silver shield. Salome seizes it.

Ah! Du wolltest mich nicht deinen
Mund küssen lassen, Jochanaan!
Wohl, ich werde ihn jetzt küssen!
Ich will mit meinen Zähnen
hineinbeißen,
wie man in eine reife Frucht
beißen mag.

Ah! You wouldn't let me
kiss your mouth, Jokanaan!
Well, I will kiss it now!
I will sink my teeth
into it,
as one bites a ripe fruit.

Ja, ich will ihn jetzt küssen
deinen Mund, Jochanaan.
Ich hab' es gesagt.
Hab' ich's nicht gesagt?
Ah! ah! Ich will ihn jetzt küssen.
Aber warum siehst du mich nicht an,
Jochanaan?
Deine Augen,
die so schrecklich waren,
so voller Wut und Verachtung,
sind jetzt geschlossen.

Yes, I will kiss it now,
kiss your mouth, Jokanaan.
I said that I would.
Didn't I say it?
Yes, yes, I will kiss it now.
But why don't you look at me,
Jokanaan?
Your eyes
that were so terrible,
so full of rage and scorn,
are closed now.

Warum sind sie geschlossen?
Öffne doch die Augen!
So hebe deine Lider, Jochanaan!
Warum siehst du mich nicht an?
Hast du Angst vor mir, Jochanaan,
daß du mich nicht ansehen willst?

Why are they closed?
Open your eyes!
Lift up your eyelids, Jokanaan!
Why don't you look at me?
Art you so afraid of me, Jokanaan,
that you won't look at me?

Und deine Zunge,
sie spricht kein Wort, Jochanaan,
diese Scharlachnatter,
die ihren Geifer gegen mich spie.
Es ist seltsam, nicht?
Wie kommt es, daß diese rote Natter
sich nicht mehr rührt?

And your tongue
says nothing now, Jokanaan,
your tongue, that was like a red snake
spitting poison at me?
That's strange, isn't it?
How is it that the red viper
moves no more?

Du sprachst böse Worte gegen mich,
gegen mich, Salome,
die Tochter der Herodias,
Prinzessin von Judäa.

You spoke evil words against me,
Salome,
the daughter of Herodias,
Princess of Judaea.

Nun wohl!
Ich lebe noch, aber du bist tot,
und dein Kopf, dein Kopf gehört mir!
Ich kann mit ihm tun, was ich will.
Ich kann ihn den Hunden vorwerfen
und den Vögeln der Luft.
Was die Hunde übrig lassen,
sollen die Vögel der Luft verzehren.

Well then!
I am still alive, but you are dead,
and your head, belongs to me!
I'm free to do with it what I wish.
I can do what I want with it;
I can throw it to the dogs and to the
birds. The birds will devour what the
dogs leave behind.

Ah! Jochanaan, Jochanaan,
du warst schön.
Dein Leib war eine Elfenbeinsäule
auf silbernen Füßen.
Er war ein Garten voller Tauben
in der Silberlilien Glanz.
Nichts in der Welt
war so weiß wie dein Leib.
Nichts in der Welt
war so schwarz wie dein Haar.
In der ganzen Welt
war nichts so rot wie dein Mund.
Deine Stimme
war ein Weirauchgefäß,
und wenn ich ansah,
hörte ich geheimnisvolle Musik.

Ah! Ah! Jokanaan, Jokanaan, you were
so beautiful.
Your body was a column of ivory
set on silver feet.
It was a garden full of doves,
and silver lilies.
Nothing in the world
was so white as your body.
Nothing in the world
was as black as your hair.
And in the whole world
nothing was as red as your mouth.
Your voice
was like a censer that scattered strange
perfumes, and when I looked at you,
I heard strange music.

Salome is lost in thought as she contemplates Jokanaan's head.

Ah! Warum hast du mich nicht
angesehn, Jochanaan?
Du legtest über deine Augendie Binde
eines, der seinen Gott schauen wollte.
Wohl!
Du hast deinen Gott gesehn, Jochanaan,
aber mich, mich, hast du nie gesehn.
Hättest du mich gesehn, du hättest mich
geliebt!

Ah! Why didn't you look at me,
Jokanaan?
You covered your eyes in order to see
your God.
Well!
You saw your God, Jokanaan, but me,
me, you never saw.
If you had seen me, you would have
loved me!

Ich dürste nach deiner Schönheit.
Ich hungre nach deinem Leib.
Nicht Wein noch Äpfelkönnen mein
Verlangen stillen.

I am thirsting for your beauty.
I am hungry for your body.
Neither wine nor apples
can ease my desire.

Was soll ich jetzt tun, Jochanaan?
Nicht die Fluten, noch die großen
Wasser können dieses brünstige
Begehren löschen.

Oh! Warum sahst du mich nicht an?
Hättest du mich angesehn,
du hättest mich geliebt.
Ich weiß es wohl, du hättest mich
geliebt.
Und das Geheimnis der Liebe ist größer
als das Geheimnis des Todes.

Herodes:
Sie ist ein Ungeheuer, deine Tochter.
Ich sage dir, sie ist ein Ungeheuer!

Herodias:
Meine Tochter hat recht getan.
Ich möchte jetzt hier bleiben.

Herodes:
Ah! Da spricht meines Bruders Weib!
Komm, ich will nicht an diesem Orte
bleiben.
Komm, sag' ich dir!Sicher,
es wird Schreckliches geschehn.
Wir wollen uns im Palast verbergen,
Herodias,ich fange an zu erzittern.

Jokanaan, what shall I do now?
Neither floods nor great waters can
ever quench the heat
of my consuming passion.

Oh! Why didn't you look at me?
If you had looked at me
you would have loved me.
I know well that you would have loved
me.
And the mystery of love is greater
than the mystery of death.

Herod: *(in a low voice to Herodias)*
Your daughter is a monster.
I tell you, she's a monster!

Herodias:
I approve of what she did.
I'll stay here now.

Herod:
My brother's incestuous wife speaks.
Come, I will no longer stay here in this
place.
Come, I tell you, that surely something
terrible will happen.
Let's hide ourselves in the palace,
Herodias, I am beginning to tremble.

The moon disappears momentarily, and then rises suddenly.

Manassah, Issachar, Ozias, löscht die
Fackeln aus!
Verbergt den Mond, verbergt die Sterne!

Manasseh, Isachar, Ozias, put out the
torches!
Hide the moon, hide the stars!

The moon disappears again, and the terrace becomes very dark.

Es wird Schreckliches geschehn.

Something terrible will happen.

Salome:
Ah! Ich habe deinen Mund geküßt,
Jochanaan.
Ah! Ich habe ihn geküßt, deinen Mund,
es war ein bitterer Geschmack auf
deinenLippen.

Salome:
Ah! I have kissed your mouth,
Jokanaan.
Ah! I have kissed your mouth.
There was a bitter taste
on your lips.

Hat es nach Blut geschmeckt?	Was it the taste of blood?
Nein? Doch es schmeckte vielleicht	No! Perhaps it is
nach Liebe.	the taste of love.
Sie sagen, daß die Liebe bitter	They say that love
schmecke.	has a bitter taste.
Allein was tut's? Was tut's?	But so what? What of it?
Ich habe deinen Mund geküßt,	I have kissed your mouth,
Jochanaan.	Jokanaan.
Ich habe ihn geküßt, deinen Mund.	I have now kissed your mouth.

A moonbeam falls on Salome, covering her with light.

Herod:

Man töte dieses Weib!

Herod: *(turning to the Soldiers)*

Kill that woman!

The Soldiers crush Salome between their shields.

End of Opera

Discography

1950   Goltz (Salome); Herrmann (Jokanaan); Aldenhoff (Herod); Karen (Herodias);
          Dresden (Saxon) State Opera Orchestra;
          Keilberth (Conductor)

1952   Wegner (Salome); Metternich (Jokanaan); Szemere (Herod);
          Von Milinkovic (Herodias); Kmentt (Narraboth);
          Vienna State Opera;
          Moralt (Conductor)

1952   Welitsch (Salome); Hotter (Jokanaan); Svanholm (Herod); Höngen (Herodias);
          Metropolitan Opera Orchestra;
          Reiner (Conductor)

1954   Goltz (Salome); Braun (Jokanaan); Patzak (Herod); Kenney (Herodias);
          Vienna Philharmonic Orchestra;
          Krauss (Conductor)

1961   Nilsson (Salome); Wächter (Jokanaan); Stolze (Herod); Hoffmann (Herodias);
          Kmentt (Narraboth);
          Vienna Philharmonic Orchestra;
          Solti (Conductor)

1963   Goltz (Salome); Gutstein (Jokanaan); Melchert (Herod); Eriksdotter (Herodias);
          Hoppe (Narraboth);
          Dresden State Orchestra;
          Suitner (Conductor)

1968   Caballé (Salome); Milnes (Jokanaan); R. Lewis (Herod); Resnik (Herodias);
          King (Narraboth);
          London Symphony Orchestra;
          Leinsdorf (Conductor)

1970   G. Jones (Salome); Fischer-Dieskau (Jokanaan); Cassilly (Herod);
          Dunn (Herodias); Ochmann (Narraboth);
          Hamburg State Opera Orchestra;
          Böhm (Conductor)

1977   Behrens (Salome); van Dam (Jokanaan); Böhme (Herod);
          Baltsa (Herodias); Ochmann (Narraboth);
          Vienna Philharmonic Orchestra;
          Karajan (Conductor)

1987   Caballé (Salome); Weikl (Jokanaan); Winkler (Herod); Dernesch (Herodias);
          Teatro all Scala;
          Nagano (Conductor)

1990   Marton (Salome); Weikl (Jokanaan); Zednik (Herod); Fassbaender (Herodias);
        Berlin Philharmonic Orchestra;
        Mehta (Conductor)

1990   Studer (Salome); Terfel (Jokanaan); Hiestermann (Herod); Rysanek (Herodias);
        Berlin Opera Orchestra;
        Sinopoli (Conductor)

1993   Ewing (Salome); Devlin (Jokanaan); Riegel (Herod); Knight (Herodias);
        Royal Opera/Covent Garden;
        Downes (Conductor)

1994   Malfitano (Salome); Pederson (Jokanaan); Zednik (Herod); Rysanek (Herodias);
        Maggio Musicale Fiorentino;
        Mehta (Conductor)

1997   Malfitano (Salome); Terfel (Jokanaan); Riegel (Herod); Silja (Herodias);
        Royal Opera/Covent Garden;
        Dohnanyi (Conductor)

1997   Nielsen (Salome); Hale (Jokanaan); Goldberg (Herod); Silja (Herodias);
        Danish National Radio;
        Schonwandt (Conductor)

Videography

DG VHS (1974)

>Stratas (Salome) Weikl (Jokanaan); Beirer (Herod); Varnay (Herodias);
>Ochmann (Narraboth); Schwarz (Page);
>Vienna Philharmonic Orchestra;
>Böhm (Conductor);
>A film by Götz Friedrich

Pioneer (1993)

>Ewing (Salome); Devlin (Jokanaan); Riegel (Herod); Knight; (Herodias);
>Leggate (Narraboth); Kimn (Page);
>Royal Opera House Orchestra;
>Downes (Conductor);
>Hall (Director);
>Bailey (Video Director)

Decca DVD (1997)

>Malfitano (Salome); Terfel (Jokanaan); Riegel (Herod); Silja (Herodias);
>Royal Opera/Covent Garden;
>Dohnanyi (Conductor)

DICTIONARY OF OPERA AND MUSICAL TERMS

Accelerando - Play the music faster, but gradually.

Adagio - At a slow or gliding tempo, not as slow as largo, but not as fast as andante.

Agitato - Restless or agitated.

Allegro - At a brisk or lively tempo, faster than andante but not as fast as presto.

Andante - A moderately slow, easy-going tempo.

Appoggiatura - An extra or embellishing note preceding a main melodic note. Usually written as a note of smaller size, it shares the time value of the main note.

Arabesque - Flourishes or fancy patterns usually applying to vocal virtuosity.

Aria - A solo song usually structured in a formal pattern. Arias generally convey reflective and introspective thoughts rather than descriptive action.

Arietta - A shortened form of aria.

Arioso - A musical passage or composition having a mixture of free recitative and metrical song.

Arpeggio - Producing the tones of a chord in succession rather than simultaneously.

Atonal - Music that is not anchored in traditional musical tonality; it does not use the diatonic scale and has no keynote or tonal center.

Ballad opera - Eighteenth-century English opera consisting of spoken dialogue and music derived from popular ballad and folksong sources. The most famous is *The Beggar's Opera,* which is a satire of the Italian opera seria.

Bar - A vertical line across the stave that divides the music into measures.

Baritone - A male singing voice ranging between bass and tenor.

Baroque - A style of artistic expression prevalent in the 17th century that is marked by the use of complex forms, bold ornamentation, and florid decoration. The Baroque period extends from approximately 1600 to 1750 and includes the works of the original creators of modern opera, the Camerata, as well as the later works by Bach and Handel.

Bass - The lowest male voice, usually divided into categories such as:

> **Basso buffo** - A bass voice that specializes in comic roles: Dr. Bartolo in Rossini's *The Barber of Seville.*

> **Basso cantante** - A bass voice that demonstrates melodic singing quality: King Philip in Verdi's *Don Carlos.*

> **Basso profundo** - the deepest, most profound, or most dramatic of bass voices: Sarastro in Mozart's *The Magic Flute.*

Bel canto - Literally, "beautiful singing." It originated in Italian opera of the 17th and 18th centuries and stressed beautiful tones produced with ease, clarity, purity, and evenness, together with an agile vocal technique and virtuosity. Bel canto flourished in the first half of the 19th century in the works of Rossini, Bellini, and Donizetti.

Cabaletta - A lively, concluding portion of an aria or duet. The term is derived from the Italian word "cavallo," or horse: it metaphorically describes a horse galloping to the finish line.

Cadenza - A flourish or brilliant part of an aria (or concerto) commonly inserted just before a finale. It is usually performed without accompaniment.

Camerata - A gathering of Florentine writers and musicians between 1590 and 1600 who attempted to recreate what they believed was the ancient Greek theatrical synthesis of drama, music, and stage spectacle; their experimentation led to the creation of the early structural forms of modern opera.

Cantabile - An indication that the singer should sing sweetly.

Cantata - A choral piece generally containing Scriptural narrative texts: the *St. Matthew Passion* of Bach.

Cantilena - Literally, "little song." A lyrical melody meant to be played or sung "cantabile," or with sweetness and expression.

Canzone - A short, lyrical operatic song usually containing no narrative association with the drama but rather simply reflecting the character's state of mind: Cherubino's "Voi che sapete" in Mozart's *The Marriage of Figaro.*

Castrato - A young male singer who was surgically castrated to retain his treble voice.

Cavatina - A short aria popular in 18th and 19th century opera that usually heralded the entrance of a principal singer.

Classical Period - A period roughly between the Baroque and Romantic periods, the late 18th through the early 19th centuries. Stylistically, the music of the period stresses clarity, precision, and rigid structural forms.

Coda - A trailer added on by the composer after the music's natural conclusion. The coda serves as a formal closing to the piece.

Coloratura - Literally, "colored": it refers to a soprano singing in the bel canto tradition. It is a singing technique that requires great agility, virtuosity, embellishments and ornamentation: The Queen of the Night's aria, "Zum Leiden bin ich auserkoren," from Mozart's *The Magic Flute*.

Commedia dell'arte - A popular form of dramatic presentation originating in Renaissance Italy in which highly stylized characters were involved in comic plots involving mistaken identities and misunderstandings. Two of the standard characters were Harlequin and Colombine: The "play within a play" in Leoncavallo's *I Pagliacci*.

Comprimario - A singer who performs secondary character roles such as confidantes, servants, and messengers.

Continuo, Basso continuo - A bass part (as for a keyboard or stringed instrument) that was used especially in baroque ensemble music; it consists of an independent succession of bass notes that indicate the required chords and their appropriate harmonies. Also called *figured bass, thoroughbass*.

Contralto - The lowest female voice, derived from "contra" against, and "alto" voice; a voice between the tenor and mezzo-soprano.

Countertenor - A high male voice generally singing within the female high soprano ranges.

Counterpoint - The combination of two or more independent melodies into a single harmonic texture in which each retains its linear character. The most sophisticated form of counterpoint is the fugue form, in which from two to six melodies can be used; the voices are combined, each providing a variation on the basic theme but each retaining its relation to the whole.

Crescendo - A gradual increase in the volume of a musical passage.

Da capo - Literally, "from the top"; repeat. Early 17th-century da capo arias were in the form of A B A, with the second A section repeating the first, but with ornamentation.

Deus ex machina - Literally "god out of a machine." A dramatic technique in which a person or thing appears or is introduced suddenly and unexpectedly; it provides a contrived solution to an apparently insoluble dramatic difficulty.

Diatonic - A major or minor musical scale that comprises intervals of five whole steps and two half steps.

Diminuendo - Gradually becoming softer; the opposite of crescendo.

Dissonance - A mingling of discordant sounds that do not harmonize within the diatonic scale.

Diva - Literally, "goddess"; generally the term refers to a leading female opera star who either possesses, or pretends to possess, great rank.

Dominant - The fifth tone of the diatonic scale; in the key of C, the dominant is G.

Dramatic soprano or tenor - A voice that is powerful, possesses endurance, and is generally projected in a declamatory style.

Dramma giocoso - Literally, "amusing (or humorous) drama." An opera whose story combines both serious and comic elements: Mozart's *Don Giovanni*.

Falsetto - A lighter or "false" voice; an artificially-produced high singing voice that extends above the range of the full voice.

Fioritura - It., "flowering"; a flowering ornamentation or embellishment of the vocal line within an aria.

Forte, fortissimo - Forte (*f*) means loud; mezzo forte (*mf*) is fairly loud; fortissimo (*ff*) is even louder; additional *fff*'s indicate greater degrees of loudness.

Glissando - Literally, "gliding." A rapid sliding up or down the scale.

Grand opera - An opera in which there is no spoken dialogue and the entire text is set to music, frequently treating serious and tragic subjects. Grand opera flourished in France in the 19th century (Meyerbeer); the genre is epic in scale and combines spectacle, large choruses, scenery, and huge orchestras.

Heldentenor - A tenor with a powerful dramatic voice who possesses brilliant top notes and vocal stamina. Heldentenors are well suited to heroic (Wagnerian) roles: Lauritz Melchior in Wagner's *Tristan und Isolde*.

Imbroglio - Literally, "intrigue"; an operatic scene portraying chaos and confusion, with appropriate diverse melodies and rhythms.

Largo or larghetto - Largo indicates a very slow tempo, broad and with dignity. Larghetto is at a slightly faster tempo than largo.

Legato - Literally, "tied" or "bound"; successive tones that are connected smoothly. The opposite of legato is staccato (short and plucked tones.)

Leitmotif - Literally, "leading motive." A musical fragment characterizing a person, thing, feeling, or idea that provides associations when it recurs.

Libretto - Literally, "little book"; the text of an opera.

Lied - A German song; the plural is "lieder." Originally, a German art song of the late 18th century.

Lyric - A voice that is light and delicate.

Maestro - From the Italian "master"; a term of respect to conductors, composers, directors, and great musicians.

Melodrama - Words spoken over music. Melodrama appears in Beethoven's *Fidelio* and flourished during the late 19th century in the operas of Massenet (*Manon* and *Werther*).

Mezza voce - Literally, "medium voice"; singing with medium or half volume. It is sometimes intended as a vocal means to intensify emotion.

Mezzo-soprano - A woman's voice with a range between soprano and contralto.

Obbligato - An accompaniment to a solo or principal melody that is usually played by an important, single instrument.

Octave - A musical interval embracing eight diatonic degrees; from C to C is an octave.

Opera - Literally, "work"; a dramatic or comic play in which music is the primary vehicle that conveys its story.

Opera buffa - Italian comic opera that flourished during the bel canto era. Highlighting the opera buffa genre were buffo characters who were usually basses singing patter songs: Dr. Bartolo in Rossini's *The Barber of Seville*; Dr. Dulcamara in Donizetti's *The Elixir of Love.*

Opéra comique - A French opera characterized by spoken dialogue interspersed between the musical numbers, as opposed to grand opera in which there is no spoken dialogue. Opéra comique subjects can be either comic or tragic.

Operetta, or light opera - Operas that contain comic elements and generally a light romantic plot: Strauss's *Die Fledermaus*, Offenbach's *La Périchole*, and Lehar's *The Merry Widow.* In operettas, there is usually much spoken dialogue, dancing, practical jokes, and mistaken identities.

Oratorio - A lengthy choral work, usually of a religious nature and consisting chiefly of recitatives, arias, and choruses, but performed without action or scenery: Handel's *Messiah.*

Ornamentation - Extra embellishing notes—appoggiaturas, trills, roulades, or cadenzas—that enhance a melodic line.

Overture - The orchestral introduction to a musical dramatic work that sometimes incorporates musical themes within the work. Overtures are instrumental pieces that are generally performed independently of their respective operas in concert.

Parlando - Literally, "speaking"; the imitation of speech while singing, or singing that is almost speaking over the music. Parlando sections are usually short and have minimal orchestral accompaniment.

Patter song - A song with words that are rapidly and quickly delivered. Figaro's "Largo al factotum" in Rossini's *The Barber of Seville* is a patter song.

Pentatonic - A five-note scale. Pentatonic music is most prevalent in Far Eastern countries.

Piano - A performance indication for soft volume.

Pitch - The property of a musical tone that is determined by the frequency of the waves producing it.

Pizzicato - An indication that notes are to be played by plucking the strings instead of stroking the string with the bow.

Polyphony - Literally, "many voices." A style of musical composition in which two or more independent melodies are juxtaposed; counterpoint.

Polytonal - Several tonal schemes used simultaneously.

Portamento - A continuous gliding movement from one tone to another through all the intervening pitches.

Prelude - An orchestral introduction to an act or a whole opera that precedes the opening scene.

Presto, prestissimo - Vigorous, and with the utmost speed.

Prima donna - Literally, "first lady." The female star or principal singer in an opera cast or opera company.

Prologue - A piece sung before the curtain goes up on the opera proper: Tonio's Prologue in Leoncavallo's *I Pagliacci.*

Quaver - An eighth note.

Range - The span of tonal pitch of a particular voice: soprano, mezzo-soprano, contralto, tenor, baritone, and bass.

Recitative - A formal device used to advance the plot. It is usually sung in a rhythmically free vocal style that imitates the natural inflections of speech; it conveys the dialogue and narrative in operas and oratorios. *Secco*, or dry, recitative is accompanied by harpsichord and sometimes with other continuo instruments; *accompagnato* indicates that the recitative is accompanied by the orchestra.

Ritornello - A refrain, or short recurrent instrumental passage between elements of a vocal composition.

Romanza - A solo song that is usually sentimental; it is shorter and less complex than an aria and rarely deals with terror, rage, or anger.

Romantic Period - The Romantic period is usually considered to be between the early 19th and early 20th centuries. Romanticists found inspiration in nature and man. Von Weber's *Der Freischütz* and Beethoven's *Fidelio* (1805) are considered the first German Romantic operas; many of Verdi's operas as well as the early operas of Wagner are also considered Romantic operas.

Roulade - A florid, embellished melody sung to one syllable.

Rubato - An expressive technique, literally meaning "robbed"; it is a fluctuation of tempo within a musical phrase, often against a rhythmically steady accompaniment.

Secco - "Dry"; the type of accompaniment for recitative played by the harpsichord and sometimes continuo instruments.

Semitone - A half step, the smallest distance between two notes. In the key of C, the half steps are from E to F and from B to C.

Serial music - Music based on a series of tones in a chosen pattern without regard for traditional tonality.

Sforzando - Sudden loudness and force; it must stand out from the texture and be emphasized by an accent.

Singspiel - Literally, "song drama." Early German style of opera employing spoken dialogue between songs: Mozart's *The Magic Flute.*

Soprano - The highest range of the female voice ranging from lyric (light and graceful quality) to dramatic (fuller and heavier in tone).

Sotto voce - Literally, "below the voice"; sung softly between a whisper and a quiet conversational tone.

Soubrette - A soprano who sings supporting roles in comic opera: Adele in Strauss's *Die Fledermaus*; Despina in Mozart's *Così fan tutte.*

Spinto - From the Italian "spingere" (to push); a singer with lyric vocal qualities who "pushes" the voice to achieve heavier dramatic qualities.

Sprechstimme - Literally, "speaking voice." The singer half sings a note and half speaks; the declamation sounds like speaking but the duration of pitch makes it seem almost like singing.

Staccato - Short, clipped, detached, rapid articulation; the opposite of legato.

Stretto - Literally, "narrow." A concluding passage performed in a quick tempo to create a musical climax.

Strophe - Strophe is a rhythmic system of repeating lines. A musical setting of a strophic text is characterized by the repetition of the same music for all strophes.

Syncopation - A shifting of the beat forward or back from its usual place in the bar; a temporary displacement of the regular metrical accent in music caused typically by stressing the weak beat.

Supernumerary - A "super"; a performer with a non-singing and non-speaking role: "Spear-carrier."

Symphonic poem - A large orchestral work in one continuous movement, usually narrative or descriptive in character: Franz Liszt's *Les Preludes*; Richard Strauss's *Don Juan, Till Eulenspiegel,* and *Ein Heldenleben.*

Tempo - The speed at which music is performed.

Tenor - The highest natural male voice.

Tessitura - The usual range of a voice part.

Tonality - The organization of all the tones and harmonies of a piece of music in relation to a tonic (the first tone of its scale).

Tone poem - An orchestral piece with a program.

Tonic - The principal tone of the key in which a piece is written. C is the tonic of C major.

Trill - Two adjacent notes rapidly and repeatedly alternated.

Tutti - All together.

Twelve-tone - The twelve chromatic tones of the octave placed in a chosen fixed order and constituting, with some permitted permutations and derivations, the melodic and harmonic material of a serial musical piece. Each note of the chromatic scale is used as part of the melody before any other note is repeated.

Verismo - Literally "truth"; the artistic use of contemporary everyday material in preference to the heroic or legendary in opera. A movement particularly in Italian opera during the late 19th and early 20th centuries: Mascagni's *Cavalleria rusticana*.

Vibrato - A "vibration"; a slightly tremulous effect imparted to vocal or instrumental tone to enrich and intensify sound, and add warmth and expressiveness through slight and rapid variations in pitch.